Reynolds – State –1985– 12.80

REAGANOMICS

BY STEPHEN GOODE
REAGANOMICS
REAGAN'S
ECONOMIC PROGRAM

A GROLIER COMPANY

Franklin Watts
New York | London | Toronto | Sydney | 1982
An Impact Book

Photographs courtesy of
United Press International Photo

Diagram p. 58, courtesy of Vantage Art

Library of Congress Cataloging in Publication Data

Goode, Stephen.
Reaganomics, Reagan's economic program.

(An Impact book)
Bibliography: p.
Includes index.
Summary: Examines the economic program advanced
by the Reagan administration, including its key-
stone, the theory of supply-side economics.
1. United States—Economic policy—1981—   —Ju-
venile literature.   2. Supply-side economics—
United States—Juvenile literature.   [1. United
States—Economic policy.   2. Supply-side economics.
3. Economics]   I. Title.
HC106.8.G66   338.973   82-2028
ISBN 0-531-04422-X   AACR2

CONTENTS

Chapter One
Crisis and Mandate
1

Chapter Two
The Enemy, Part I
15

Chapter Three
The Enemy, Part II
27

Chapter Four
The Conservative Attack
43

Chapter Five
The Reagan Economic Program
65

Chapter Six
The Reagan Victory
79

Chapter Seven
The Confrontation with Reality
93

Chapter Eight
Critics Right and Left
107

Suggested Further Reading
115

Index
117

REAGANOMICS

CHAPTER
1
CRISIS
AND
MANDATE

Many Americans today, just as they did 200 years ago, feel burdened, stifled, and sometimes even oppressed by government that has grown too large, too bureaucratic, too wasteful, too unresponsive, too uncaring about people and their problems.

Ronald Reagan on the eve of the presidential election of 1980.

The 1970s were a period of growing economic crisis in the United States. Inflation was rampant, and no one seemed to know what to do about it. Unemployment remained uncomfortably high. The constant parade of statistics and figures produced by government agencies and private researchers remained gloomy and pessimistic. Hopeful periods of recovery were short-lived and followed by renewed recession and uncertainty.

The economic crisis of the 1970s contrasted vividly with the prosperity of the previous two decades. Between 1948 and 1973, the productivity of American employees increased by an average of 2.9 percent annually—an increase that allowed a steady growth in real wages and the development of higher standards of living. In 1970 the median American family was 64 percent wealthier than it had been twenty years earlier.

The prosperity of the 1950s and 1960s was unprecedented. Americans spent more and saved more than they had in the past. Energy was cheap and social planners and visionaries spoke of a time to come when poverty and need would disappear. The American Dream—a home, a car or two, a decent job, and college for the children—seemed to be in the grasp of almost everyone.

It was this dream that the crisis of the 1970s threatened to destroy. Inflation was regarded by most Americans as the most serious problem. In 1973 it reached 13 percent, far higher than it had been in recent memory. By 1979 it had become 18.2 percent and many feared it might go higher.

Government officials tended to blame the high rate of inflation on the high cost of energy after 1973, owing to an enormous increase in the price of oil by OPEC, the organization of oil-producing countries. But many economists argued that the inflation was caused by a number of factors, including high government spending and the rapid rise in the national debt.

But whatever its cause, the effects of inflation were experienced by all Americans. Prices climbed rapidly, making it more difficult to feed a family on current salary levels. The value of savings went down. The purchase of a home or a car became out of the question for a growing number of people in the middle class. For the poor and for people on fixed incomes, inflation was cruelest of all.

Coupled with "double-digit inflation"—as it was dubbed by the press—was the stagnation of the economy. Together, the two pernicious economic forces were called "stagflation." In the 1970s the productivity of the American economy began to decline. There was still growth in the economy, but that growth was painfully slow and this slow rate of growth meant that the economy was not expanding rapidly enough to provide new jobs or to compete meaningfully with the economies of other capitalist nations.

Stagnation too meant that businessmen were less likely to undertake new business ventures. "There is that peril in our society," noted Thomas A. Murphy, the chairman of General Motors, "the unwillingness to take a reasonable risk." But without risk, there would be no economic expansion, no progress.

Another characteristic of the 1970s was the growing rate of unemployment. The unemployment rate in the United States rose by 75 percent between 1973 and 1975 for a total of 8 percent of the "experienced" work force. It fell after that, fluctuated, and rose again at the end of the decade. Unemployment was lowest among white males, but among other groups, such as black teenagers, it reached as much as 90 percent.

By the end of the decade interest rates were at near-record levels. The prime lending rate at major banks—the rate at which these banks loaned money to their best customers—rose to 20 percent and above and remained high for long periods of time. This made it difficult for Americans to purchase homes or cars or for businessmen to take out loans to expand their businesses, buy new equipment, or improve their plants. The "tight-money" policy was adopted to help bring down inflation, but in bringing down inflation it also slowed down the economy and contributed to the economic stagnation characteristic of the 1970s.

Symbolic of the economic crisis that afflicted the nation were the problems of New York City and the Chrysler Corporation. Both the city and the corporation were representative of American greatness: New York, the leading metropolitan area, and the center of banking, the communications industry, and other enterprises; Chrysler, a major car manufacturer, with a name known throughout the world.

Yet, in the late 1970s, both were on the verge of bankruptcy and both called upon the federal government for help in time of crisis. Critics blamed New York's fiscal irresponsibility for its troubles and pointed out that Chrysler had failed to adapt to a market where smaller foreign cars were increasingly popular. But clearly, if the economic crisis could affect giants like these, then the crisis was of major proportions.

The United States did not experience the economic downturn of the 1970s alone. Inflation and other economic problems likewise afflicted dynamic economies like those of Japan, West Germany, Sweden, and France, as well as those of communist nations. The economic crisis was world-wide and reflected the international character of economic life. What affected one nation affected others as well, and no nation could hope to remain immune to the downturn.

In the late 1970s, there was a proliferation of books like Paul Erdman's *The Crash of '79* (1976) predicting imminent catastrophe. Many of these works offered dire, sometimes hysterical, accounts of impending doom. But respected and academic economists also shared in the gloom. Left-of-center economist Robert Heilbroner, a professor at the New School for Social Research in New York, opened his 1978 book *Beyond Boom and Crash* with the statement: "Another worldwide crisis of capitalism is upon us."

In 1980 Princeton University Press published a closely-argued economic analysis by Manuel Castells entitled *The Economic Crisis and American Society*. Castells, who is professor of city and regional planning at the University of California at Berkeley, agreed with Heilbroner:

The shadow of the crisis spreads over the world. Beyond the effects of temporary variations of the business cycle, the daily life of people in most countries is being shaped by the economic crisis of the 1970s and its lasting effects on the world capitalist system.

According to Castells, some of the manifestations of the crisis were "closed factories, empty offices, millions of unemployed, days of hunger, declining cities, crowded hospitals . . . fearful stock markets." But he also listed another manifestation: "stunned economists"—stunned because no one seemed to know how to deal with the crisis or where it might lead.

In his 1981 book, *Wealth and Poverty*—which President Reagan regards as a profound expression of his own economic beliefs—conservative George Gilder wrote that the result of the stagnation of the 1970s was an "economy of frustration." Americans were frustrated because they could no longer buy what they wanted to buy or live at the level of affluence they had once enjoyed. The economic problems of the 1970s, Gilder said, were "devastating on Americans of all classes," and had led to the "demoralization" of the elite—the wealthy Americans who controlled the money and whose investments determined economic growth and prosperity.

For some observers, the crisis portended the end of capitalism, which they believed had come to the end of its creative and expansive abilities. For others, however, the crisis was man-made, and therefore could be solved by man. Jan Tumler, the chief economist of the world trade organization GATT (General Agreement on Tariffs and Trade) argued that "the 1980s must be a period of rethinking the functions of government. We should figure out what governments should do and can do well and what governments should not even try to do."

Francois de Combret, the economic adviser to President Giscard d'Estaing of France, was likewise levelheaded and encouraging. In 1980 de Combret declared: "There is nothing European investors want more now than to invest in the U.S. The reason is your capitalist system. Your crisis is caused not by the system but by the workings of the system. When an engine breaks down you don't call the principle of internal combustion into question. You fix or replace the engine."

Even Robert Heilbroner, who at times has been a strong critic of capitalism, concludes his *Beyond Boom and Crash* on an optimistic note. The Marxist economists and others who predict an end to capitalism, he wrote, do not understand the capitalist system.

History has shown capitalism to be an extraordinarily resilient, persisting, and tenacious system, perhaps because its driving force is dispersed among so much of its population rather than concentrated solely in a governing elite. In pursuit of the privileges, the beliefs, and above all the profits of capitalism, its main protagonists have not only created the material wonders

[7]

that Marx marveled at, but shown a capacity for changefulness that even he, who never underestimated the self-preserving drive of capital, did not fully anticipate.

In spite of this optimism, however, the crisis of the 1970s remained and continued to grow. Would capitalism make use of its amazing recuperative powers to overcome its present stagnation, as Heilbroner suggested it might? Would Americans follow the advice of economist Jan Tumler and use the period of the 1980s as a time to rethink the role of government in economic life? These were questions that took on great significance as the new decade opened and played a major role in the presidential campaign of 1980.

Mandate for Change
By the end of February 1980 the administration of President Jimmy Carter had grown deeply concerned about the economy. Past efforts the administration had made to bring the economy under control were not working. Inflation and interest rates stood above 18 percent and were spreading dissatisfaction and fear throughout the country. Moreover, it was an election year and President Carter realized that unless there was a major economic turnaround in the next few months, his chances for reelection were dim.

For three weeks, the White House worked hard to develop a convincing economic plan. Prominent businessmen and economists were invited to give their views on the crisis. Congressmen of both parties were consulted regularly to impart their opinions on what Congress might be willing to do to stimulate the economy.

On Friday, March 14, President Carter delivered a major economic address to a group of invited guests at the White House. "Persistent high inflation threatens the economic security of our country," Carter said. "This dangerous situation calls for urgent measures." What has to be done, he concluded, is that "the Federal Government must stop spending money we do not have and borrowing to make up the difference."

[8]

The president announced his intention to balance his proposed budget for fiscal 1981, which would begin on October 1, 1980. Six weeks earlier, his proposed budget had included a deficit of $15.8 billion, but now the president believed that that was too large for the economy to tolerate. The last president to maintain a balanced budget successfully* had been President Johnson in fiscal 1969, eleven years earlier. A balanced budget in 1980, Carter believed, would show the American people and the world that his administration was serious in its attack on inflation.

Throughout his speech, President Carter called for "discipline." There should be "discipline by reductions in the Federal Government," he said, meaning that he planned to cut government spending. There should likewise be "discipline by greater conservation of energy" and "discipline by restraints on credit," he added, and proposed a new gasoline tax and new curbs on consumer borrowing.

After his speech, the president held a press conference. "The Federal Government," he explained, "simply must accept discipline on itself as an example for others to follow." He recognized that his program would be "difficult politically"—in an election year Congress would be reluctant to pass bills that might anger the public—and that cuts in government spending would prove "onerous and burdensome" to the poor and needy. But unless the government brought inflation under control, he claimed, future suffering would be far greater than any suffering spending cuts might now entail.

The president's program, however, was too little and too late. It alienated liberals in his own party who believed that cuts in social programs were cruel and unnecessary. The liberal ADA (Americans for Democratic Action) called it "a cruel deception of the people" and throughout the country, the ADA and other liberal organizations vowed to oppose it.

*The successful balanced budget of fiscal 1969 was begun under the Johnson administration and concluded by President Nixon. There was a surplus of $3.2 billion at the end of that fiscal year.

More important, however, was the fact that Carter's program failed to convince the nation that the administration was serious in its drive for a better economy. President Carter already worked under a label of ineptness—in the press and elsewhere he was widely regarded as a man not "up" to the office of the presidency—and there was concern that he would not prove strong enough to see his program through. From a very high approval rating during his early days in office, President Carter's popularity had fallen to a rating of 20 percent by 1980—the lowest level any president had achieved since the pollsters began to take their polls.

The central elements of Carter's program—the balanced budget and the call for spending cuts—were staples of conservative economic doctrine. But conservative as they may have been, they were not sufficiently conservative for the man who emerged as Carter's chief Republican opponent in the presidential campaign, Ronald Reagan, the former governor of California.

Reagan attacked the Carter administration as the "failed presidency" and called for vigorous new leadership that would lead the country out of economic stagnation. In his acceptance speech for the Republican nomination for president, he charged that "thanks to the economic policies of the Democratic Party, millions of Americans find themselves without work." Under his administration, he claimed, those policies would come to an end.

In the same speech, Reagan also leveled an attack at Carter's tax policies. President Carter, he charged, had overseen the largest increase in taxes in American history, yet he asks the American people to have the discipline to do with less. Has the president thought, Reagan asked, "about those who have always had less? This is like telling them that just as they step on the first rung of the ladder of opportunity, the ladder is pulled out from under them."

But Reagan directed his strongest words against big government. Big government, he warned, is "never more dangerous than when our desire to have it help us blinds us to its great power to harm us." Americans, he implied, have too long relied on government as a source of security and well-being and must once again learn to rely on their own abilities and initiative. What we must have, he concluded, is "the clarity of vision to see the difference between what is essential and what is merely desirable, and then the courage to bring our Government back under control."

Late in the summer of 1980, as the presidential campaign began to heat up, Carter received bad news about the economy. His program had failed to create a turnaround. Statistics released by federal agencies showed that the economy had slumped in the second quarter of the year by a rate of 9.1 percent—a rate of decline unequalled by any since World War II. In addition, inflation had risen to 10.5 percent during the same period, up a whole percentage point from the first three-month period of 1980. These figures meant that there would be a sharp decline in Americans' "real" take-home pay—pay that has been adjusted after inflation is taken into account.

What was Reagan's answer for the continuing economic crisis? The Reagan economic program was a mixture of old conservative doctrine and new ideas developed by a group of young conservatives called the "supply-side" school of economics. On the one side, the program called for a balanced budget and for decreased government spending. On the other, it called for a vast decrease in the taxes paid by businesses and individuals.

The program appeared in speeches made by Reagan and in statements and position papers issued by his campaign aides. First and foremost, as could have been expected, the program directed its attention at big government. Big government, Reagan believed, was at the root of America's economic decline. Big government spent too much, and thereby sent the inflation rate soaring, causing money to lose its value and threatening the well-being of the nation.

One solution, therefore, was to cut big government down in all possible ways. This could be done by decreasing the number of bureaucrats and by cutting numerous government programs. During the campaign, Reagan mentioned two departments he believed government could do without: energy and education, both of which had been established during the Carter administration.

Reagan also argued that big government led to "waste, fraud, and mismanagement." If these three problems could be eliminated, he maintained, then huge sums of money could be saved that would otherwise go down the drain. The savings, he claimed, would be phenomenal—enough to help the government pay many of its debts. On October 28, a week before the election, Reagan said:

> . . . most people when they think about cutting government spending, they think in terms of eliminating necessary programs or wiping out something, some service that government is supposed to perform. I believe that there is enough extravagance and fat in government . . . one of the Secretaries of H.E.W. under Mr. Carter testified that he thought there was $7 billion worth of fraud and waste in welfare, and in the medical programs associated with it. We've had the General Accounting Office estimate that there are probably tens of billions of dollars lost in fraud alone, and they have added that waste adds even more to that.

One area where Reagan believed that government should not cut back, but should expand its activities was defense. The Soviet Union, he said, had attained a dangerous military superiority over the United States, and that superiority had to be eliminated. The Reagan economic program therefore called for enormous increases in government spending for defense.

Candidate Reagan also argued that big government led to over-regulation of the economy. Government regulations, he was fond of pointing out, covered 20,000 pages in 1970, but had nearly quadrupled in a decade to reach 77,498 pages in 1979. He called for "a thorough and systematic review of the thousands of Federal regulations that affect the economy," contending that in many cases "regulations have gone to extremes and become counterproduc-tive." Excessive regulation, he said, hampered business activity and industrial production and was responsible for much of the stagnation the economy was experiencing.

Where Reagan parted company with traditional conservative economic policy was in his call for a tax cut. He supported the controversial Kemp-Roth tax bill, which had been defeated in Congress. The Kemp-Roth bill asked for a 30 percent decrease in taxes over a three-year period. Reagan believed that this tax cut—which would be the largest ever undertaken in American history—would prove to be a stimulus to the economy.

The tax cut, Reagan argued, would stimulate the economy by making available to businessmen and others vast new sums of money that would otherwise have gone to the government. This money could be used to reinvest in business and industry, leading to an expansion of the economy. An expanded economy, in turn, would provide new jobs for the unemployed and lead to an increase in the amount of taxes the government collected. Eventually, the money lost due to the tax cut would be replaced by the taxes taken from the expanding economy.

There was also a moral basis to Reagan's economic program. The program was designed not only to reinvigorate the stagnating economy, but also to reinvigorate the American spirit. Time and time again, Reagan mentioned how big government had developed a sense of "dependence" on the part of Americans, and had destroyed traditional values such as self-reliance and individual initiative. Hard work, he said, had made America great and wealthy, and if America were to survive its present economic dilemma, it would have to return to its traditional values.

During the last months of the campaign, Reagan held separate television debates with President Carter and Independent party candidate John Anderson. Anderson, a Republican congressman from Illinois who had left his party because he could not support Reagan's policies, directed one of his most challenging questions at Reagan's economic program. How was it possible, Anderson asked, to raise defense spending, cut taxes, and balance the budget, all at the same time?

In his answer, Reagan fell back on his belief in supply-side economics. The tax cut, he said, would lead to an expanded economy which would generate new income to pay for defense and balance the budget. And there would also be the savings his administration would generate from cutting back on waste and fraud. He repeated his confidence in his economic program and his belief that it was the only program any candidate had put forth that was powerful and imaginative enough to solve the economic crisis.

In a debate with President Carter, Reagan scored what may have been his greatest triumph of the campaign. Reagan asked Americans to ask themselves if they were better off in 1980 than they had been four years earlier when Carter took office. If they were, Reagan implied, then they should vote for Carter. If they weren't, then they should vote for him.

When the votes were counted, Reagan won by a landslide. He received 489 electoral votes to Carter's 49. Carter had carried six states and the District of Columbia; Reagan had carried 44. Reagan received 51 percent of the popular vote; Carter, 41 percent; and Anderson, 8 percent.

Was it a mandate for the policies Reagan had articulated during the campaign? Political analysts were uncertain. Many argued that it was as much a rejection of Carter's "failed presidency" as an endorsement of Reagan and his programs. Nevertheless, the president-elect accepted the election as a mandate for change and set about to prepare for a reshaping of American society according to his vision.

In the next chapters, we shall look closely at Reagan's economic program. First we shall look at the liberal tradition of "big government" which Reagan wanted to uproot and destroy. Next, we shall turn to the program itself, discussing its details and the origin of its ideas and concepts. Finally, we shall see how that program has worked during the first year of Reagan's presidency.

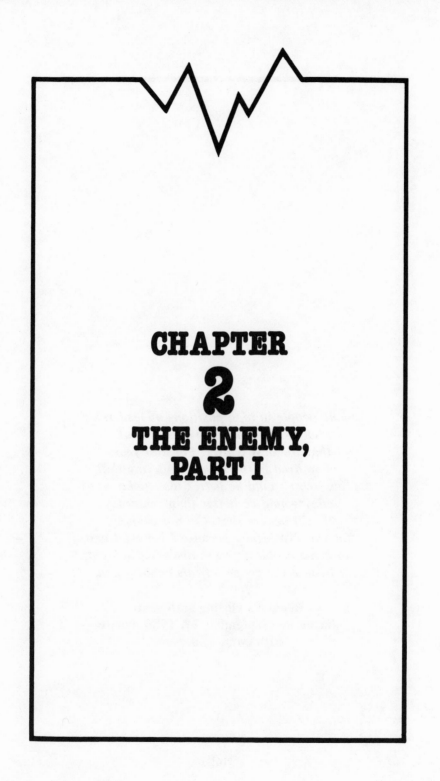

CHAPTER
2
THE ENEMY, PART I

*Some people in high positions of leadership
tell us that the answer is retreat,
that the best is over. For 200 years
we've lived in the future, believing that
tomorrow would be better than today and
today would be better than yesterday.
I still believe that. I'm not running
for the Presidency because I believe I can
solve the problems we've discussed tonight.
I believe the people of this country can.*

**Reagan's closing statement
during his September 21, 1980 debate
with John Anderson.**

The enemies that Reagan's economic program seeks to defeat are, of course, inflation, unemployment, and the stagnation of the economy. But behind these problems lies what Reagan regards as the real enemy: fifty years of mistaken and wrong-headed policies that have led to big government and the welfare state.

For Reagan and his followers, the United States took a wrong turn in the 1930s that resulted in a vastly overinflated bureaucracy and an economy that no longer works. The wrong turn came during the presidency of Franklin Roosevelt and was known as the New Deal.

President Hoover and the Great Depression

On March 4, 1929, President Herbert Hoover offered an optimistic picture of American society in his inaugural address. "If we survey the situation of our Nation at home and abroad," Hoover said, "we find many satisfactions."

Ours is a land rich in resources; stimulating in its glorious beauty, filled with millions of happy homes; blessed with comfort and opportunity. In no nation are the institutions of progress more advanced. In no nation are the fruits of accomplishment more secure.

Hoover spoke at the end of a decade, the 1920s, in which economic prosperity had improved the lives of many Americans. The standard of living was higher than it had ever been; the American economy was the most productive on earth. Unfortunately all that was soon to come to an end. The security and progress Hoover mentioned in his speech were about to be profoundly shaken.

On October 29, 1929, eight months after Hoover took office, the American stock market collapsed. The repercussions of that collapse were felt around the world. Beginning slowly at first, the Great Depression soon gained momentum. By 1932 twelve million Americans—one out of every four in the work force—were unemployed. By 1933 the GNP (Gross National Product, the total production of the economy) was almost one-third less what it had been in 1929. Every twenty or thirty years in the past, the American economy had suffered setbacks or depressions, but the Great Depression was by far the worst of them all.

More than eleven thousand banks closed their doors. Millions lost their savings and their homes, farms, or businesses. Hunger was widespread and breadlines long. The Great Depression dampened the spirits of many Americans who could no longer provide adequate shelter, clothing, or food for their families or find meaningful employment. Never before had the American Dream been so undermined by economic reality.

What was government to do in this crisis? At first little or nothing. President Hoover, hoping to encourage the American people, promised that "prosperity was just around the corner" and that "we have now passed the worst." As the Depression grew far deeper and lasted long-

[18]

er than anyone in the administration had predicted, the secretary of labor announced to the country: "Courage and resource are already swinging us back on the road to recovery. And we are fortunate in having a President who sets us a shining example of that courage and initiative."

In Hoover's own party, the Republican party, there were two schools of thought on what the government should do about the Great Depression, the conservatives and the progressives. The conservatives agreed with the secretary of the treasury, Andrew Mellon, one of the richest men in America, who believed that it would be best to let everything alone, and the Depression would work itself out.

In many ways, Mellon regarded the Great Depression as a good thing. As a result of the economic hardship the country now faces, he said, "people will work harder, live a more moral life. Values will be adjusted and enterprising people will pick up the wrecks from less competent people." Republican progressives, opposed to Mellon's views, urged the president to use the government to provide jobs for the unemployed and to relieve the misery that was spreading across the country.

President Hoover first tried Mellon's approach. The president was a deeply compassionate man, but he was loathe to use the federal government as an instrument to institute social and economic change. Such notions, he believed, would destroy American freedom and liberty and lead to the creation of an all-powerful state.

During World War I and the early 1920s, as a private citizen, Hoover had organized a vast program of relief that brought food, clothing, and other essentials to war-torn Europe and later to the Soviet Union. Now, as president, he called upon the churches and private charities of America in the winter of 1929–1930 to undertake an enormous drive for funds to relieve the victims of the Great Depression. The charity drive was a failure and gathered only $15 million—far short of the amount needed.

Later in his administration, Hoover acknowledged the need for government intervention. He approved a program

[19]

of public works and public construction that would help put people to work again. He also approved a program of loans to insurance and mortgage companies, railroads and industries, and other businesses that faced bankruptcy.

No American president had ever made such an extensive use of government to relieve the private sector of the economy or help those who had suffered from the Depression. But, warned Hoover, experimentation with the role of government in private affairs should be made cautiously and temporarily. "Any change of policies," he added, "will bring disaster to every fireside in America."

Many Americans, however, looked upon Hoover's program—as radical as it was for its time—as a program that primarily benefited the rich. Will Rogers, the most popular political satirist of his day, had words to describe it. "The money" the president offered the nation, Rogers said, "was all appropriated for the top in the hopes it would trickle down to the needy." The phrase stuck. From then on, any government program that seemed to benefit business or the wealthy over the masses of people would be called "trickle-down theory" and would be derided as relief for the rich and pennies for the poor.

Enter Franklin Roosevelt

In 1928 Hoover had defeated his Democratic opponent for the presidency, Alfred Smith, by a landslide. The Great Depression, however, quickly undermined the popularity he had enjoyed. The Democrats successfully, but unfairly, labeled the Depression "Hoover's Depression," and managed to place the blame for the economic crisis squarely on the shoulders of the discredited president.

At their Chicago convention in the summer of 1932, the Democratic party nominated Franklin Roosevelt, the governor of New York, to run against Hoover in the November election. During his acceptance speech before the assembled delegates, Roosevelt declared, "I pledge you, I pledge myself, to a New Deal for the American people." Roosevelt then attacked the inactivity of the Hoover administration and said that, if elected president, he would address himself directly to the problems of the people.

Roosevelt had pledged himself and his party to a "New Deal," but during his campaign he offered no radical departures from past government policy. His economic program sounded quite conventional. He spoke of the need for a balanced budget to restore the credit of the United States and of other traditional plans to create economic stability. There was little hint of the "revolution" he was to initiate once he was in office.

Roosevelt was elected by a landslide of greater proportions than Hoover's victory over Smith four years earlier. On March 4, 1933, he became president. It was during the famous first "one hundred days" of his administration that the proportions of the New Deal and of the changes he planned for the country became clear. If Hoover had made unprecedented use of the federal government to relieve the economic crisis, Roosevelt made even far greater use of it.

During his first one hundred days in office, Roosevelt proposed several tradition-breaking government programs he hoped would improve the economy and put people back to work. Among the most significant were the following:

• *The Emergency Banking Act*. Passed by Congress in a record eight hours, this bill provided for the reopening of the banks then closed throughout the country. It likewise gave the treasury department authority to prevent the hoarding of gold and to issue more currency. On the Monday following the passage of the bill, the banks reopened.

• *The Civilian Conservation Corps (CCC)*. The CCC was a means to get unemployed young men to work. By mid-June, 1933, thirteen hundred CCC camps had been set up under army control. By August 300,000 young men were at work. Before the camps were closed during World War II, more than two and a half million young men had worked in CCC projects, which included the reforestation of seventeen million acres of land, the construction of dams to prevent soil erosion, and other similar projects.

• *The Abandonment of the Gold Standard.* Perhaps the most economically controversial element of the New Deal was the announcement that the United States was going off the gold standard, as Great Britain had done two years earlier. The move deeply troubled conservative Americans because it broke the unspoken contract between the government and the public that money would be backed by gold. Nevertheless, the abandonment of the gold standard helped to stimulate foreign trade.

• *The Federal Emergency Relief Act.* This bill appropriated $500 million, later increased to $5 billion, for direct relief to states, cities, towns, and counties. A new bureaucracy, the CWA (Civil Works Administration), grew out of it. By January 1934 the CWA had more than four million people on its roles and was eventually to have more than 400,000 projects under way throughout the country—public parks, schoolhouses, roads, airports, and similar public works.

• *The Work Projects Administration (WPA).* The WPA spent billions on reforestation, rural electrification, water works, slum clearance, and scholarships for students, among other projects.

• *The Agricultural Adjustment Act and the Emergency Farm Mortgage Act.* These bills helped to alleviate the plight of farmers, who had been harder hit by the Depression than other groups in American society. As a result of measures provided by the bills, national farm income increased from $5.6 billion in 1932 to $8.7 billion in 1935.

• *The Glass-Steagall Banking Act.* This bill required banks to get out of the investment business and placed

[22]

severe restrictions on the use of banking funds for speculation. It likewise offered a federal guarantee for individual bank deposits, to assure that savings and other money held in banks would not be lost in future depressions.

Also passed during the first one hundred days of Roosevelt's first administration were an Economy Act, the Securities Act, the Home Owner's Loan Act, the National Industrial Recovery Act, and the Tenessee Valley Authority Act—all designed to restore faith in the depressed economy, to put people back to work, and to raise the standards of living of many who had fallen on bad times.

In 1935 new programs were added to the New Deal. The Revenue Act of 1935—sometimes called the "soak the rich" law—vastly increased the amount of taxes the wealthy were required to pay, reaching 79 percent on incomes over $5 million. Also adopted was the Social Security Act, whose aim was to secure "the men, women, and children of the nation against certain hazards and vicissitudes of life." Included in the program were benefits for the aged, the infirm, dependent mothers and children, and unemployment insurance.

The New Deal and American Society
Conservatives denounced the New Deal as an unwarranted intrusion by the government in affairs that should have remained private. Some claimed it was communist inspired, others that it was fascist. It was neither. Roosevelt took no steps to nationalize any sector of the economy, or any other move designed to transform American capitalism into something else. Indeed, the president defended his program as necessary to preserve the American system, not to destroy it.

In March 1937, in his second inaugural address, Roosevelt defended the New Deal:

In this nation, I see tens of millions of its citizens—a substantial part of the whole population—who at this

[23]

very moment are denied the greater part of what the very lowest standards today call the necessities of life. I see millions of families trying to live on incomes so meager that the pall of family disaster hangs over them day by day. . . . I see one-third of a nation ill-housed, ill-clad, ill-nourished.

It was these problems, the president said, which explained his philosophy of government intervention. His administration believed that its responsibility was more than to oversee an end to the Depression or relieve the immediate problems of Americans. Roosevelt went on:

Our covenant with ourselves did not stop there. Instinctively we recognized a deeper need—the need to find through government the instrument of our united purpose to solve for the individual the ever-rising problems of a complex civilization. Repeated attempts at their solution without the aid of government had left us baffled and bewildered. . . . We refused to leave the problems of our common welfare to be solved by the winds of chance and the hurricanes of disaster.

"In this," he concluded, "we Americans were discovering no wholly new truth; we were writing a new chapter in our book of self-government."

Roosevelt never gave a clearer picture of the purpose of the New Deal. Beyond a solution to the Depression, government was to provide a blanket of security around Americans, to protect them from economic want and insecurity. It was to make life more comfortable and easy, less precarious and hazardous. If the government wouldn't do it, then who would?

Economists debate whether the New Deal was successful in bringing an end to the Great Depression. There are arguments on both sides of the issue. In 1940, seven years after Roosevelt came to power, more than 8.7 million workers were still unemployed in the private sector. Other economic indicators likewise cast doubt on any significant improvement of the economy until the United States entered World War II in 1941 and the nation geared up for war.

On the other side of the argument, however, was the fact that the New Deal had raised the national income from $40.3 billion in 1933 to $72.6 billion in 1939, surely a significant achievement. But more important, perhaps the most significant contribution the New Deal gave to American society was psychological, and therefore unmeasurable. At a time when many Americans had lost faith in government and American institutions, the New Deal offered hope. At a time when the national outlook was gloomy and pessimistic, it had sought to restore confidence and optimism.

The contrast between the Hoover administration and the Roosevelt era reflects a basic dichotomy in American history. On the one hand, America has offered its citizens economic freedom—the right to establish an enterprise, carry it through to fruition, and enjoy the rewards of hard work. Economic freedom has been regarded as the underpinning of all the other freedoms and liberties enjoyed by Americans. Without economic freedom, it is argued, and the diversity and pluralism it creates, there would be no freedom of the press, no freedom of religion, and so on.

On the other hand, America is also a nation that prides itself on its democratic tradition and its belief in equality. In times of extreme economic crisis like the Great Depression, however, the contrast between the drive for equality and the right of economic freedom becomes vivid. In times of economic crisis, the fact that many Americans are not equal to others becomes painfully obvious, while the fact that some are better able to cope than others becomes equally clear.

The problem for government, in such instances, is to decide which tradition to emphasize: economic freedom or the drive for equality. The Hoover administration chose economic freedom, believing it was thereby defending the most basic American traditions. The Roosevelt presidency opted for the tradition of equality and emphasized that the chief duty of government was "to provide for the general welfare"—a phrase found in the Preamble to the Constitution.

Roosevelt's liberalism had a profound effect on American history. During the New Deal and afterward, the government's role in the relief of economic distress and unemployment was vastly enlarged. Expanded too was the government's part in the physical rehabilitation of the country and in the preservation of natural resources.

But more significantly, under Roosevelt and afterward, economic and social planning by the government became an established part of American life. Corporations and other businesses had carefully planned for the future for years, but Americans had always been suspicious of government planning, regarding it as somehow inferior or more dangerous than planning in the private sphere. The New Deal helped make government planning more acceptable to many Americans.

The expansion of the federal government under Roosevelt was reflected in the rapid increase in the bureaucracy. In 1932 there had been 600,000 civilian federal employees; in 1940 there were more than a million. After 1941 the tradition of big government begun by the New Deal would snowball as government expanded to meet the needs of World War II and later the Cold War.

Thus the enemy the Reagan economic plan sought to destroy had its origins in the 1930s, in Roosevelt's massive efforts to relieve economic misery and provide a blanket of security for all Americans. It was at that point, Reagan believed, that the nation had made its wrong turn—away from the tradition of economic freedom toward a drive for equality and state protection. Now was the time to set the balance between the two traditions aright and to give economic freedom its proper sphere of action in American life.

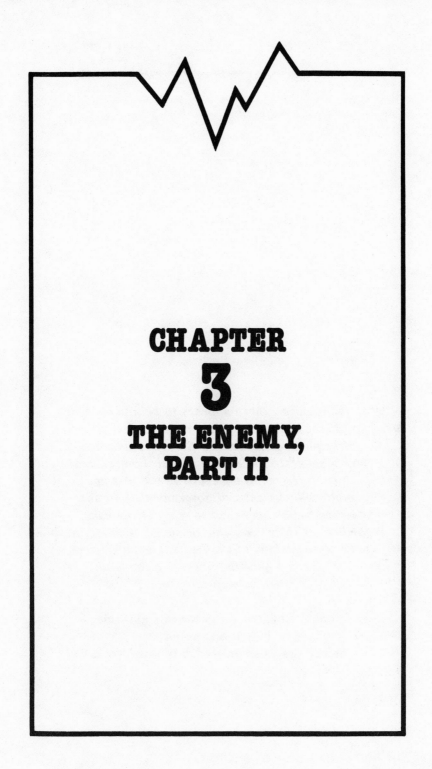

CHAPTER
3
THE ENEMY,
PART II

*At the moment, there appears to be a panic fear
afloat in the air, partly due to a feeling
of helplessness, a feeling that government is
now a separate force beyond their control, that
their voices echo unheeded in the vast and
multitudinous halls of government. I do not
remember a time when so many Americans,
regardless of their economic or social standing, have
been so suspicious of the Federal establishment.
There is a question abroad in the land:
"What is happening to us?"*

**Ronald Reagan, Governor of California,
in a 1968 speech
before the Economic Club of New York.**

The 1930s saw the arrival of big government in the United States. They likewise saw the appearance of a major new economic theory which defended government intervention in the economic life of capitalist countries. The theory came from England and was the product of John Maynard Keynes, a brilliant Cambridge University economist.

Keynes' revolutionary work, *The General Theory of Employment, Interest and Money* (1936), appeared too late to exert much influence on the New Deal. President Roosevelt was never converted to Keynesian economics and throughout his presidency indicated his dissatisfaction with continued large deficit spending practices. After World War II, however, Keynesian economics began to play an important role in Washington. Before long, its emphasis on government planning and government stimulation of economic growth became the dominant economic philosophy in government circles.

The Keynesian Theory

Before Keynes published his "general theory," most economists believed that all the goods produced by a capitalist economy would find a market. Public demand would seek out these goods and purchase them, thereby stimulating the production of more goods. Thus, given sufficient time, a market was assured for all that was produced, and if a market was there for all goods that were produced, it meant that a capitalist economy had a built-in mechanism which saved it from self-destruction.

But more than that. If a market was assured for all goods that the capitalist economy produced, capitalism must be a system where expansion and growth were natural and perpetual. The production of more goods led to greater demand which led to the production of more goods and a higher level of demand and so on, with no end in sight.

What troubled Keynes about this traditional model of how the capitalist system works was that it did not explain the longevity of the Great Depression. What bothered Keynes was not so much the causes of the Depression itself, but why the capitalist system continued to exist so long in a state of stagnation, with no improvement and no visible sign of a recovery from the ruins of the economic crisis.

After 1929, Keynes noted, the economies of the major industrial nations of Europe and North America tended to stand still. The factors necessary to increase output were there—idle factories, machines and equipment, and a large unemployed work force—but they were not put to use. The natural expansiveness of capitalism did not come to the rescue of the system and renew the productivity and health of the economy.

To explain this phenomenon, Keynes first pointed to a contradiction in capitalist philosophy. In normal times, savings were regarded as a good thing and people were urged to save. Savings helped increase investment power and led to economic expansion. In times of economic stagnation, however, if everyone followed this advice and saved or hoarded his or her money, then no money would be available for investment to create future wealth. The problem, then, was to find a way to unleash savings, so that economic stagnation was broken and expansion was possible.

Keynes also noted a second characteristic of the stagnation of the Great Depression. This was the pessimistic outlook of most businessmen. The entrepreneurs of the 1930s, Keynes explained, had no faith in the future expansion of the economy and therefore held back from using their savings or acquiring loans to spend for expansion. Their pessimism destroyed their initiative and desire to play a creative role in the economy. At the same time, their failure to play their traditional role in the economic sytem kept that system in a state of equilibrium, reinforcing their pessimistic outlook on the future.

Keynes did not stop to analyze the psychological reasons for the pessimism of the entrepreneurs. Rather, he concentrated on what could be done to destroy that pessimism and replace it with optimism. What could be done to stimulate the creative endeavors of the businessman, he asked? What could be done to create sufficient confidence that would cause those with skill, ability, and wealth once again to have faith in the system and to work within it?

At this point, Keynes argued, the role of government became essential. Traditionally, governments had responded to economic depression by raising taxes or reducing public spending. But this was wrong, he said, for by these measures governments "simply threw their constituents out of work and failed to balance the government's own budget." Traditional conservative economic programs, he believed, were simply not adequate to meet the problems raised by the Great Depression.

Keynes concluded that an alert and concerned government, by taking proper measures, could help tame the depressed business cycle and alleviate the miseries of its victims. He supported a wide range of government planning and expenditure. In a time of crisis, he argued, the government should not spend less, but more—in programs designed to stimulate the creative capacities of the people and insure future economic expansion.

Such spending, Keynes said, was not to be wild and uncontrolled. To be beneficial and worthwhile, it had to be rational, and to be rational, it had to be carefully thought out and monitored. Careful government planning and control by economic experts were essential. Otherwise chaos and increased economic insecurity would result, not renewed prosperity.

Keynes, however, was neither socialist nor communist. He detested Marxism or any ideology and held deep contempt for the Soviet Union. He wanted to preserve capitalism, not destroy it. Capitalism, he believed, provided the basis for the good society because it left open the possibility of personal choice and contributed to the "variety of life."

Keynesian economics endowed the state with the prime responsibility of securing capitalism against disaster. But it did not regard the state as the final cause of prosperity. Government helped create a climate of economic optimism and well-being; the individual businessman and entrepreneur who took advantage of that climate to create new economic expansion was the real hero of the Keynesian system.

The Continued Growth
of Big Government

In England, Keynes had praised Roosevelt in 1933 for taking America off the gold standard. A proponent of managed currencies, he called the move "magnificently right." In 1934 Keynes visited Roosevelt at the White House and recommended deficit spending as a solution to the economic crisis. "Nothing else counts in comparison with this," he had said.

Four years later, in 1938, Keynes wrote Roosevelt a letter and once again urged massive deficits to put people back to work and spur the economy. But Roosevelt proved reluctant to take the advice. By Keynesian standards, the government spending provided by the New Deal was too small to solve the enormous problems raised by the Great Depression.

If the president remained unconvinced by Keynesianism, others in the government were not. During World War II, the government rapidly increased deficit spending to help pay for the war effort. The result was total employment of the work force and a level of production never before attained by the United States. World War II seemed to prove the Keynesian model for economic success.

Moreover, World War II was waged, both at home and abroad, by a program of vast government planning. Young Keynesian economists were found in the treasury department and were scattered through other agencies, including those that had been established especially to deal with wartime control: the Office of Price Administration (OPA) and the War Production Board (WPB).

These young economists applied careful Keynesian analyses to problems of raw materials, labor, and the capital available to handle wartime problems. The Nobel Prize–winning American economist Paul Samuelson has written that the high level of work carried on by the economists in Washington resulted in a high level of economics in the American government, markedly superior to the quality of German economics.

The Keynesians, however, turned their attention not only to the problems necessary to win the war, but, after 1943, to the problems of peacetime prosperity that would follow the war. A number of government planning agencies—from the Bureau of the Budget (now the Office of Management and Budget, or OMB) to the National Resources Planning Board and the National Housing Agency—produced plans for postwar government activity.

Perhaps the most interesting plan was that produced by the National Resources Planning Board. The NRPB was purely a producer of ideas; it had no control over the allocation of government funds. Nevertheless the plan it produced indicated the direction the government would take in the future.

The NRPB plan favored an improved and enlarged program of Social Security, continuing programs of public works, and government efforts to redistribute wealth. Its plan also listed a New Bill of Rights, which featured several Keynesian elements. The first five points of the New Bill of Rights were the most interesting:

1. The right to work, usefully and creatively, through the productive years.
2. The right to fair pay, adequate to command the necessities and amenities of life in exchange for work, ideas, thrift, and other socially valuable service.
3. The right to adequate food, clothing, shelter, and medical care.
4. The right to security, with freedom from fear of old age, want, dependency, sickness, unemployment, and accident.
5. The right to live in a system of free enterprise, free from compulsory labor, irresponsible private power, arbitrary public authority, and unregulated monopolies.

The NRPB envisioned a whole new set of responsibilities government should assume for the well-being of American citizens. In 1944 the Democratic party platform partly endorsed this vision by going beyond the immediate goals of the New Deal to announce that government had the duty "to guarantee full employment" to all Americans when the war ended. It was the first time a Keynesian goal had been adopted by a major American political party.

In February 1946, six months after the end of World War II, Congress adopted a Maximum Security Act. The bill passed after long debate and committed the federal government to a program that would utilize the nation's resources to the fullest to insure "maximum employment, production and purchasing power."

The bill directed the president to develop a "general program" for "Federal investment and expenditure" that would stimulate "private business, consumers, State and local governments" to rise "to the level required to assure full employment volume of production." It also established a Council of Economic Advisers to keep the president informed about current business and economic trends and to recommend measures that might be taken to maintain economic expansion and to soften recession.

The council's power was limited to recommendation; the president was not bound by the advice he received. Nevertheless, the Maximum Security Act of 1946 showed that Congress had moved in the direction of accepting the necessity of government planning and direction of the economy. It likewise showed that Keynesian theory had made a deep inroad in the American consciousness.

One result of the adoption of Keynesian notions of government planning was that the power of Congress over budgeting problems declined, while that of the president increased. Congress, with its numerous members, was ill-equipped to agree on economic policy. The executive branch, on the other hand, armed with the Bureau of the Budget and other executive agencies, had the power and expertise to organize and control government spending in response to the needs of the economy, thereby regulating the economic pattern of American society.

Congress had the power to modify the budget through its taxing and appropriation privileges, but the chief power and responsibility over the budget belonged to the president. "The managed economy, in short, offered new forms of unilateral power to the President who was bold enough to take action on his own," wrote Samuel Lubell in *The Future While It Happened* (1973). An advance in the power to plan the economy was therefore an advance in presidential power.

Truman and Eisenhower
The administration of President Harry Truman worked within the tradition of Roosevelt and Keynes; President Eisenhower tried to break with that tradition. Truman

called his expansion of New Deal policies the Fair Deal. The Fair Deal supported an increase in minimum wages and expanded Social Security benefits, extending them to ten million Americans who had previously been ineligible to receive them. It also began a new housing program directed at slum clearance and the construction of 800,000 units of low-income housing.

By 1950, near the end of Truman's presidency, however, a major reaction had set in to the expanded role government was playing in social and economic affairs. The New Deal was now almost two decades old, the Great Depression over, the war won, and a growing prosperity was spreading across the country. The problems the New Deal was designed to overcome seemed long past and there was a growing call for less government intervention, less government spending, and less government activity.

Opposition to the New Deal tradition came to center in one man, Dwight Eisenhower, the Republican candidate for president in 1952. Eisenhower called his approach to government "dynamic conservatism," which, he believed, could provide progress without an expanded role for government. He believed that one of his chief duties as president would be to "clean up" what one of his closest aides called "that mess in Washington" that Roosevelt had made and Truman had compounded.

Eisenhower was elected president by a landslide. In his autobiographical book, *Mandate for Change* (1962), Eisenhower wrote that he regarded his impressive victory as a mandate from the American people to reverse "trends which were twenty years old." Government power, he believed, should be scaled down and made more human. Washington did not have an answer for every problem.

In the book Eisenhower also wrote of his distaste for those who advocated "centralization" and greater government power. Such people, he claimed, believe they are "infallible." Moreover, "they liked power, and they lacked faith in the people." It was faith in the people—in their ability to chart the courses for their own lives, free of gov-

[36]

ernment intervention—that Eisenhower wanted to restore.

The Eisenhower program for the economy included balanced budgets and prudent fiscal policy. Attacking government intervention in the economy, Eisenhower's secretary of the treasury said, "I believe with all my heart in an incentive free enterprise system." Attacking Keynesian notions of deficit spending, the secretary of commerce warned: "You can't spend your way to riches."

During eight years in office, however, Eisenhower was unable to reverse the trend toward big government. The bureaucracy continued to grow. In 1953 Eisenhower created the Department of Health, Education, and Welfare (HEW), with a budget of $2 billion. The new department was soon to become one of the most rapidly expanding divisions of the executive branch. But it was not alone; other government agencies also increased their manpower and authority during the Eisenhower years.

Nor did Eisenhower oversee an end to the New Deal. With his approval, Congress passed a new and improved Social Security law. It also raised the nationwide minimum wage and extended unemployment compensation to cover an additional four million workers. In 1955 Congress added a moderate public housing program to the responsibilities undertaken by government.

Moreover, the fiscally prudent Eisenhower was able to balance the budget only three times—in 1955, 1956, and 1960—during his eight-year tenure in office. The liberal Harry Truman, by contrast, had balanced the federal budget four times during his seven-year presidency. Under Eisenhower, federal deficits and the federal debt increased, inflation appeared, and there was a major recession and lagging economic growth.

The Great Society
The next major confrontation between the advocates of government intervention and those who believed in economic freedom came during the 1964 presidential contest

[37]

between Barry Goldwater and Lyndon Johnson. Goldwater was a conservative senator from Arizona, author of the popular anti–big government book, *The Conscience of a Conservative* (1960). Johnson had become president in November 1963 upon the assassination of John Kennedy.

Throughout the campaign, Goldwater ardently defended the conservative cause. He accused many of his fellow Republicans of "me-tooism," meaning that they joined the Democrats in supporting increased government spending and an increased role for the federal government in the economy. With me, Goldwater claimed, "you have a choice, not an echo."

Johnson, on the other hand, was a strong advocate of New Deal liberalism. As a freshman congressman, he had come to Washington during the Roosevelt years and had stood firmly in the Roosevelt tradition since that time. He believed that government had a positive role to play in the establishment of the American Dream.

Goldwater lost decisively, carrying only six states to Johnson's forty-four. President Johnson proceeded to carry out what he had already begun upon the death of President Kennedy: the establishment of what he called "the Great Society," a series of government programs he hoped would complete what the New Deal had begun thirty years earlier.

Johnson's program took interesting forms. In 1964 he signed into law a tax cut that had been proposed by President Kennedy. The tax cut lowered income taxes for individuals and for businesses. It was an experiment, based on Keynesian economics, designed to encourage businessmen by lowering their taxes. And it worked. Following the enactment of the cut, business activity expanded and the economy improved.

Johnson also declared an "unconditional war on poverty in America." In 1964 Congress appropriated $950 million for ten separate antipoverty programs to be supervised by the Office of Economic Opportunity (OEO), an agency established as part of the executive office of the president.

A Job Corps to train underprivileged young people, a work-training program, an adult education program, and a program to guarantee loans to establish small businesses were included. In addition, VISTA (Volunteers in Service to America) was established to bring needed skills and expertise to depressed and backward areas of the country.

In 1965 and 1966 the Great Society was completed by a landslide of government programs:

• *The Elementary and Secondary Education Act* appropriated $1.3 billion in federal aid to school districts throughout the United States. Also, $2.3 billion was appropriated for federal loans to college students and aid to higher education.

• *Head Start and Upward Bound programs* were added to the OEO agenda. Head Start was directed toward preschool age children from deprived families. Upward Bound was designed to prepare talented poor young people for college.

• *Medicare amendments to the Social Security Act* provided hospital insurance and certain types of hospital care for virtually all Americans on reaching age sixty-five.

• *Other new programs* established assistance for the redevelopment of eleven depressed states in Appalachia, the "beautification of highways," the purification of smog-laden air, the restoration of polluted waterways, and the regeneration of cities smitten by "urban blight" and the deterioration of housing.

Under Johnson, government intervention in economy and society reached new heights. But Johnson waged two wars. In addition to his war on poverty, he expanded America's role in the Vietnam War. The result was a severe strain on the economy. Believing that the nation could afford both "guns and butter," Johnson increased federal spending to pay for both. In 1965 the federal debt stood at $317 billion. In 1970, after Johnson had left office, it was $370 billion.

A Theorist of Big Government

The most articulate defender of an extended government role in the economy and society in recent years has been John Kenneth Galbraith, now professor emeritus of economics at Harvard. Galbraith developed his thesis in three best-selling works, *The Affluent Society* (1958), *The New Industrial State* (1967), and *Economics and the Public Purpose* (1973).

The theme of Galbraith's economic trilogy is clear. "Left to themselves," he writes, "economic forces do not work out for the best except perhaps to the powerful." In order for an economy to work and to work well and justly, it needs guidance and careful planning; otherwise, only the wealthy and well-placed will benefit.

Galbraith rejects entirely the notion that government should step back and let the economy function freely. "One cannot have a socially excellent economic system," he claims, "without having an economic system." And the failure to establish a socially excellent economic system, he concludes, is almost always the result of "policies that are in the interest not of the many but of the few" carried out under "the pretense that it is the many who are being served." In other words, the trickle-down theory simply does not work to establish a fair economic system.

Galbraith takes issue with what he calls the "conventional wisdom" that guides the government in economic matters. Many of the ideas conservatives use to shape American social and economic policy, he argues, were shaped in periods of relative poverty and scarcity. These ideas are the "conventional wisdom" that tells conservatives that the economy is best-served when the government stands back and refuses to intervene.

But for many years now, Galbraith points out, America has been an affluent society, where the old, traditional

[40]

"conventional wisdom" no longer holds. What is needed, he adds, is the development of new ideas to meet the new conditions American society is experiencing.

American prosperity, Galbraith goes on, is due in large part to the existence of large corporations which are able to exert enormous economic power. These corporations are wealthy and well-organized, with power comparable to small nations. But corporations, Galbraith says, act only in their own interest and cannot be relied upon to consider the benefit of the nation as a whole or the well-being of the majority of American citizens.

Destroying the corporations, Galbraith argues, is out of the question. The result would be economic chaos and uncertainty. What is needed, he believes, is something more powerful than the corporations that could rein in the self-interest of the giant corporations and force them to consider the welfare of the nation. And this force, Galbraith maintains, could only be the federal government in Washington.

By careful planning and the exertion of federal power, Galbraith concludes, an economic system can be established that serves the best interests of all citizens. But a crucial element in the system, he adds, is an informed electorate, willing to make its interests known and capable of influencing the government to act in its behalf. The government can aid in the establishment of economic justice, but only when the people make their demands known. Otherwise, Galbraith fears, the enormous power of the corporations will dominate American economic life and American politics.

The discussion of the origins and development of big government in the past two chapters has served to underline the vast task Reagan has set himself in his economic program. Fifty years of government economic momentum, from the New Deal to the Great Society and onward, cannot be easily undone. For many years now, the government has played an important role in giving economic security to

[41]

millions of Americans, and Americans have come to rely on that role and to expect the government to act in times of crisis.

The difficulty of Reagan's task is likewise underlined when the fate of the two Republican presidents who followed Lyndon Johnson is considered. Both Richard Nixon and Gerald Ford criticized big government—but did nothing to stop its momentum. Under these two middle-of-the-road Republican presidents, the social and economic programs begun during the Great Society experienced their periods of greatest expansion.

By 1978, the year after Gerald Ford left office, the budget of HEW, which administers many social programs, had reached $160 billion—more than one and one-half times the total expenditures for the army, navy, and air force. President Nixon, long regarded as an economic conservative, had publicly declared himself to be a Keynesian and had used Keynesian principles to aid the economy.

Thus the problem for President Reagan and his economic program is to undo not only the wrong turn he believes was taken under President Roosevelt, but also to abandon policies accepted by presidents of his own political party. His decision to undo the work of the past can only be regarded as revolutionary. Reagan believes that fifty years of big government have led to the present economic stagnation. But he must also ask himself if big government has not also had a role in creating the prosperity that has characterized American life for so long.

CHAPTER
4
THE
CONSERVATIVE
ATTACK

No nation can grow and adapt to change except to the extent that it is capitalistic, except to the extent, in other words, that its productive wealth is diversely controlled and can be freely risked in new causes, flexibly applied to new purposes, steadily transformed into new shapes and systems.

George Gilder, *Wealth and Poverty* (1981).

By the 1960s and 1970s the heritage of the New Deal and Keynesian economics seemed to many Americans an accepted part of life. But there was still an undercurrent of conservative thought which challenged this belief. It appeared during the Eisenhower administration and again in the unsuccessful presidential campaign of Barry Goldwater in 1964, when it went down to defeat in the Johnson landslide.

But with the end of the economic boom of the 1960s and the subsequent economic uncertainty of the 1970s, conservative criticism of liberal government policy began to take deeper root. By 1980, when conservatism emerged triumphant in the presidency of Ronald Reagan, it had called into question every government program that had sprung up during the New Deal and afterward.

The conservatives attacked the costs of big government, believing them unreasonable and extravagant. They likewise charged that big government led to fraud, waste, and mismanagement, and they were able to find numerous instances of these problems to prove their point. But beyond the charges of cost and waste, the conservatives also argued that the government programs to improve the economy and society were failures and had not achieved what they had been designed to do.

Inflation

Reagan has called inflation "the cruellest tax of all." In finding a cause for the rampant inflation of the 1970s, he and the conservative economists whose views he shares blamed government spending. "Government causes inflation," Reagan declared in Amarillo, Texas, during the 1980 campaign. "We've got to make the government make it go away."

What arguments did the conservatives have to bolster their contention that government caused inflation? The basic problem, the conservatives believed, was that government now guaranteed a minimal standard of economic performance. But due to the nature of the political system, that minimum standard could not remain static, but had to increase each year to satisfy the demands of Americans.

Congressmen and presidents could not promise more of the same. To stay in office they had to promise—and provide—ever-increasing levels of economic performance. Since the accepted philosophy behind big government was "the more government action, the better," government increased its spending to improve economic performance. The result was that inflation was pushed ever higher.

Moreover, there was an inertia about government that prevented it from "cleaning its own house." Once a government program was adopted, it was kept regardless of failure or success. And most government programs had a life of their own, increasing their spheres of activity and demanding ever-increasing funds for expenditure.

Thus conservatives believed that the results of big government had been the creation of an inflationary spiral, for which the government was responsible, and which would continue to grow as long as the government stood by the policies it had followed for almost half a century. The only

[46]

way for the nation to move out of the economic spiral, Reagan believed, was to abandon the economic principles that had created it.

"The Welfare Mess"

Had welfare improved the lot of America's poor and destitute? Had it helped them survive and face the future with encouragement? Reagan believed that it had not. In speech after speech, both during his presidential campaign and as president, he pointed to private charity as a better means to relieve the misery of the truly needy. Private charity, he maintained, helped to preserve human dignity and made the poor less dependent on government help.

The conservative argument against welfare was developed by Charles Hobbs in his book *The Welfare Industry* (1978), published by the Heritage Foundation, a strong supporter of Reagan's policies. Welfare, Hobbs contended, did not provide help to people who wished to rise from poverty into a productive life. Rather it gave people a more than adequate excuse to remain in poverty and on welfare.

Welfare recipients received checks that were graded to rise with the inflation rate. They likewise received Medicaid and other government benefits that helped them cope with the problems of daily existence. If all these benefits were lumped together, Hobbs said, they amounted to an income of $15,000 for a family of four in 1976, which had risen to nearly $18,000 by 1978.

During the same period, he pointed out, the median income of an average American family had risen from $14,500 to $16,500. Thus a welfare family could expect to receive more income if it remained on welfare than if the breadwinner of the family went into the job market. The lavish benefits bestowed by welfare, Hobbs concluded, provided no incentive for self-improvement and change.

Welfare, the conservatives believed, had made what should have been a temporary problem—the sustenance of a family until a job could be found—into a permanent problem. The children of parents on welfare were likely

[47]

themselves to look to the welfare system for support when they matured. The welfare system, the conservatives concluded, was creating generation after generation of hopelessness and unproductive lives.

Housing Subsidies

Beginning with the New Deal, the government provided subsidies to aid in slum clearance and the construction of low- and middle-income housing. In 1965, during President Johnson's drive for the Great Society, the Department of Housing and Urban Development was established to oversee government housing programs.

These programs, the conservatives argue, have been a conspicuous failure. More housing has been destroyed than has been built. Moreover, much of that which has been built has deteriorated quickly, owing to tenant misuse and lack of responsibility, into large numbers of unusable and abandoned units.

The conservatives believe too that the government's housing programs have tended to benefit not those who need housing but those who make profits building housing. Thus a March 21, 1979 article in the *Wall Street Journal* revealed that the chief thrust for the construction of government subsidized housing came from "contractors, bankers, labor unions, materials suppliers," and others, and not from the poor and needy.

The *Wall Street Journal,* which was quoting a study made by the Federal Trade Commission, went on to say that as soon as the contractors and others had been paid for their services, they no longer took an interest in the project. The government too loses interest and the result is "leaky roofs, inadequate plumbing, bad foundations," and other problems that are never corrected.

The Creation of Jobs
by the Government

Government programs to create jobs, the conservatives point out, are popular and politically attractive because they are ways to "get people off the streets" and into a position to play a productive role in society. Roosevelt's New Deal had programs designed to put people to work, and every liberal administration since Roosevelt has followed suit. In 1979 the Carter administration approved the appropriation of $12 billion for a jobs program of unprecedented size and scope.

The problem with these programs, say the conservatives, is that the jobs they create are an illusion. They supply little meaningful work and give the worker little or no sense of accomplishment or satisfaction. Moreover, they are generally unproductive. To prove their contention, the conservatives point to numerous studies which show that young people and others who hold government-created jobs find them unsatisfactory.

The conservatives stress their belief that the government cannot *create* jobs. It merely utilizes the wealth it has gleaned from the private sector to finance jobs. In the end, all government-created jobs depend on the stability and productivity of the private economy.

Unemployment Insurance

The problem with unemployment insurance, the conservatives say, is that it is used for all the wrong purposes. In an article entitled "The Economics of the New Unemployment" in the Fall 1973 issue of the conservative journal, *The Public Interest*, Martin Feldstein argues that unemployment insurance actually promotes and encourages unemployment.

Workers eligible for unemployment benefits, Feldstein claims, frequently take off work to take advantage of those benefits. The compensation they receive is often high and amounts to a significant portion of their original income. They can use their free time as a vacation or secretly to find another job, which will make their total income higher than ever before. Similarly, the conservatives believe, disability insurance may aid many people who are genuinely disabled, but also it can be taken advantage of by many others with minor injuries, who choose to magnify their problems beyond their immediate seriousness.

[49]

The Moral Collapse
of Liberalism

The conservatives applied the arguments described in the preceding pages to every social and economic endeavor undertaken by big government. Such endeavors, they believed, were costly mistakes, and invariably failed to solve anything. But the conservative attack on liberalism cut more deeply than that. For at the core of liberal thinking, the conservatives concluded, lay a profoundly erroneous and distorted view of mankind and the world.

The welfare state provided a "cradle to grave" blanket of security and social insurance for Americans. It provided protection from life's vicissitudes and attempted to improve the lot of the poor and needy. But in so doing, the conservatives claimed, the welfare state had made life devoid of meaning.

Conservative writers found that a primary failing of liberalism was its failure to understand human psychology. Human beings, they tell us, thrive on risk and adventure, not on security and inactivity. Life is a struggle and hard work a reality. Moreover, in order to improve their condition and develop, human beings must be in a position they will fight to overcome. This is "the way the world works," conservative journalist Jude Wanniski tells us in his book *The Way the World Works* (1978).

The trouble with the welfare state was that it made people dependent. It made them dependent on government programs and "handouts," on the largesse of politicians and the whims of bureaucrats. This state of dependency, the conservatives believed, took away incentive, ambition, initiative, and drive. Instead of saying "I shall do it," Americans had become prone to say "let the government do it for me."

Liberalism was morally decadent, the conservatives argued, because it had but one answer to the problems that plagued society: more government. But with every increase in government power, human freedom and liberty decreased. The conservative writers of the 1970s were fond of looking back to a 1944 book by the Nobel Prize–winning Austrian economist Friedrich von Hayek, entitled *Road to Serfdom*. In that book, von Hayek had argued that government planning and control were tempting alternatives for governments to pursue, but in them lay the danger that governments would eventually become all-powerful and people mere "serfs."

In their book *Free to Choose* (1979) and their public television series of the same name, Milton Friedman, also a Nobel Prize–winning economist, and his wife Rose developed the same thesis. "The combination of economic and political *power* in the same hands," they wrote, "is a sure recipe for tyranny." When the political arm of society, the government, also assumes control of the economy, the result can only be a despotic state. "Economic freedom," they claimed,

> *is an essential requisite for political freedom. By enabling people to cooperate with one another without coercion or central direction, it reduces the area over which political power is exercised. In addition, by dispersing power, the free market provides an offset to whatever concentration of political power may arise.*

This was the way the economy should work, the conservatives said. Not as an arm of the state, but as a separate entity, powerful enough and sufficiently independent that it could challenge the government's political power when that power became excessive.

One of the most complete statements of the new conservatism appears in George Gilder's *Wealth and Poverty*. Gilder opens his book with the statement, "The most important event in the recent history of ideas is the demise of the socialist dream." Wherever governments have attempted to put the socialist dream into practice, he claims, the result has been widespread dissatisfaction.

Gilder believes that there is a basic contradiction built into the socialist—and liberal—ideal. Socialism and liberalism, he points out, argue that rational state planning can

[51]

produce a rational and predictable world. Fifty years of state planning, he maintains, have proved that this is not so. But even if a rational and predictable society were attainable, he adds, it would not be a desirable society because it would be a society without innovation or change.

"A world without innovation," Gilder writes, "succumbs to the sure laws of deterioration and decay." Thus the ideal socialist state would carry the seeds of its own destruction. Lack of movement, he implies, is movement backward. The wise society is one that preserves and nourishes its sources of growth and progress.

For Gilder, the only system that provides for genuine growth and progress and helps maintain forward momentum is capitalism. A capitalist system that is allowed to work, he believes, creates incentive, develops ambition, and destroys the feelings of dependency rampant in the welfare state. Gilder contrasts the "stationary economy," which he believes we have now, with his ideal free economy:

Only in a stationary economy can government no longer defer to scientists, technologists, and businessmen as the heroes of the age. In the stationary state all that matters are the works of power and bureaucracy: mass behavior and its regulation. Conservation, distribution, and control become the crucial values. Economists, too, come into their own. Without the surprises of creativity, their models can actually predict the future.

The capitalist economy, on the other hand, unleashes creativity and welcomes it, according to Gilder. It is not afraid of unpredictability and change. It turns its back to the advice of bureaucrats and planners, allowing the people who really understand economic growth and progress— Gilder's "heroes of the age," businessmen, technologists, and scientists—to put their ideas and ambitions into practice.

For too long, Gilder concludes, liberalism has been the dominant economic and political philosophy in America.

[52]

Capitalists and conservatives have been taught to feel shame for the ideas they hold. It is now time, he adds, for Americans to abandon fifty years of wrong ideas and to adopt the conservative dream of the ideal society.

President Reagan has spoken warmly about Gilder's book and views. Although published too late to have a direct influence on Reagan's economic program, *Wealth and Poverty* nevertheless expresses the basic ideas behind that program. How does Reagan propose to get the "dynamic, creative forces" of capitalism working again? In the next chapter, we shall turn to Reagan's plans, and look at them closely.

Above: President Roosevelt signs the Social Security Act, an important program of the New Deal that continues to provide benefits to millions of elderly and disabled Americans. *Opposite:* during the Hoover Administration in 1931, men and women who were out of work marched in Washington, D.C., to demonstrate for unemployment insurance.

**Lady Bird Johnson is shown here in a film
designed to attract volunteers to work in the
Head Start Program that President Johnson
began during his war on poverty in the 1960s.**

These senior citizens were among the first
to sign up for Medicare benefits shortly
after the legislation was passed in 1966.

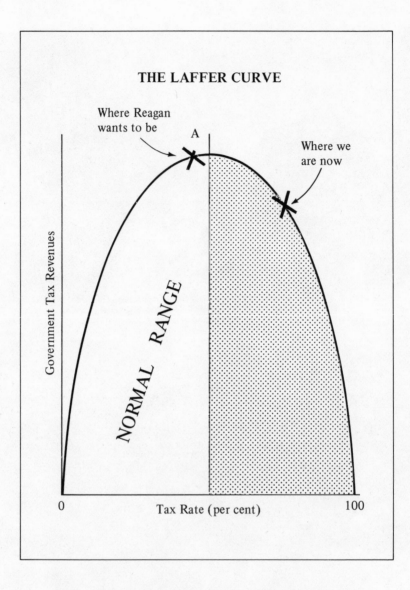

The Laffer curve indicates the relationship between tax rates and the amount of money collected by the government in revenue. The theory is that increasing tax rates produces increased revenue up to a point near A on the diagram. After that point, continued increases in tax rates result in a drop in revenue.

President Reagan poses with the book
*America's New Beginning: A Program
for Economic Recovery*—the volume
that outlined the economic program
he presented to a joint session of
Congress on February 18, 1981.

**President Reagan reviews his budget message
while some of his top economic aides look on.
Standing behind the President are, from the left,
Treasury Secretary Donald Regan, Chairman of the
Council of Economic Advisers Murray Weidenbaum,
Assistant to the Director for Budget Review
Dale McOmber, and OMB Director David Stockman.**

**Before a hearing of the Senate Finance Committee,
Budget Director David Stockman chats with
Senator Russell Long (D-La.), Senator Robert
Dole (R-Kans.), and Senator Harry Byrd (I-Va.).**

**Proposed changes in the Social Security Act
brought a storm of protests such as this one
staged by senior citizens in San Francisco.
The proposal was defeated in the Senate 96-0.**

For Americans such as these waiting on line
in an unemployment office in Detroit, Michigan,
will the Reagan economic plan restore stability
and prosperity to the economy, as the supply-side
economists believe? Or will it mean a catastrophic
decline in employment, as liberal critics fear?

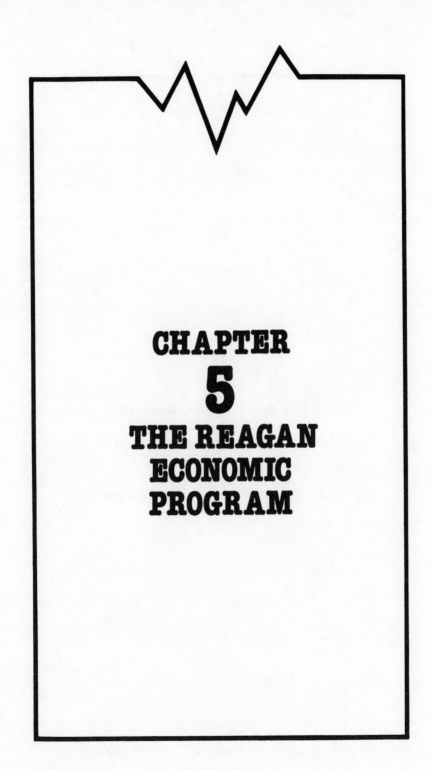

CHAPTER
5
THE REAGAN
ECONOMIC
PROGRAM

*The weakness of the inducement
to invest has been at all times
the key to the economic problem.*

John Maynard Keynes,
***The General Theory of Employment,
Interest and Money***

On September 9, 1980, during the presidential campaign, Republican officials issued a position paper entitled "Ronald Reagan's Strategy for Economic Growth and Stability in the 1980s." The paper was drawn up by a group of prominent economists who advised Reagan on economic matters, including Alan Greenspan and George Schultz, and emphasized the importance of providing "predictability" and confidence in a strong economic future to businessmen and consumers alike.

The plan lists five major interlocking parts. The aim of a Reagan administration, it explained, would be (1) to limit "the rate of growth of government spending to a reasonable, prudent level," (2) to reduce "personal income tax rates and accelerating and simplifying depreciation schedules in an orderly, systematic way in order to remove the increasing disincentives to work, to save, to invest, and to produce," (3) to undertake "a thorough review of regulations that affect the economy and prompt action to change those to encourage economic growth," (4) to establish "a

[67]

stable and sound monetary policy," and (5) to restore "confidence by following a consistent national economic policy that does not change from month to month."

The plan reflected two schools of economic thought among Reagan's advisers. One approached the economy in a traditionally conservative manner which John Kenneth Galbraith might call the "conventional wisdom." The other was a group some observers have called the "radical conservatives," who called themselves the "supply-side" school of economics and advocated a new approach to bring about economic improvement.

The "Conventional Wisdom"

On the traditional side, the position paper advocated reduced government spending leading to a balanced budget, vigorous control of waste, fraud, and mismanagement, increases in defense spending, and a decrease in federal regulations. These were familiar conservative goals, supported by the Eisenhower administration in the 1950s and defended by Barry Goldwater in the campaign of 1964.

"We must move boldly and decisively," the document said, "to control the runaway growth of Federal spending." In his campaign speeches, Reagan rejected Keynesian deficit spending, citing the example of family expenditure. Just as a family cannot continue, year after year, to spend more than it earns, his argument ran, so the federal government cannot continue deficit spending and adding to the national debt. The desired goal of "fiscal integrity" required the government to pay its debts and cease borrowing to cover its extravagances.

To bring down federal spending, candidate Reagan said that as president he would order an immediate freeze on the hiring of federal employees. He also said that he would begin to eliminate "waste and fraud" from government programs, which would lead to a savings of $64.4 billion by 1985. According to the *Wall Street Journal* on October 24, 1980, some "waste and fraud" cuts would be cost-of-living increases in Social Security benefits, repealing the minimum wage, allowing states to abolish their food-stamp programs, and cutting off federal housing aid to cities with rent control laws.

During his campaign, Reagan said little about monetary policy, but here too the statements he made were within traditional conservative doctrine. He called for a "sound, stable and predictable monetary policy" and promised to nominate to the Federal Reserve Board "men and women who share his commitment to restoring the value of the American dollar." He did not mention it, but such a policy committed him to continued high interest rates in order to bring down inflation and increase monetary value.

The "conventional wisdom" also led Reagan to endorse plans to bring down government regulations. He proposed a requirement that any new regulations be accompanied by an "economic impact statement" so that the benefits of the regulations could be weighed against the effect they would have on jobs and the economy. As for regulations already on the books, Reagan announced that his administration would have the task of "analyzing every Federal regulation" under its jurisdiction "to see if these regulations are needed."

Reagan believed that the most important single item in his budget would be an increase in defense spending. He called for an improved nuclear missile force, the early development of the MX missile, the building of the B-1 bomber and strategic cruise missiles, and a modernized air defense system. His defense plans, he recognized, would be expensive and would require vast increases in government money.

The Laffer Curve
The Reagan economic program also endorsed enormous cuts in individual income taxes—10 percent each year for three years for a total cut of 30 percent—and at this point, he moved away from traditional conservative policy. Reagan's tax policy was based on a new economic concept, called the Laffer curve, which purported to show that large

[69]

tax cuts would have an enormous stimulative effect on the economy, shaking it out of its doldrums.

According to one story, the Laffer curve originated one evening in 1974 at the Two Continents Restaurant in Washington, D.C. Three men—Arthur Laffer, a young economist; Jude Wanniski, an editorialist for the *Wall Street Journal*; and Richard Cheney, a White House aide of President Ford—were discussing the current economic slump that had struck the nation. Laffer argued that federal taxes had become so high that they had begun to discourage investment, thus holding back any meaningful expansion of the economy. If the high tax rates were slashed, he maintained, the economy would react immediately, employment would go up, and investments would soar.

At that point, Laffer is supposed to have drawn a curve on a napkin to illustrate his argument. The Laffer curve was bell-shaped. At either end of the curve were the points at which the government could bring in no tax revenues. At one end was the zero rate of taxation, where the government required no tax payments. At the other was the 100 percent taxation rate, which would bring in no tax revenue because it would bring a quick halt to all taxable activity.

At the top of the curve, where the curve crested, was the point of "maximum revenue." At this point, the government reached the peak of its ability to tax profitably. Any increases beyond this point would lead to a decrease in taxes taken in because business would cease to have sufficient incentive to expand, business profits would fall, and there would be less income for the government to tax. The high point on the curve was where taxation began to act as a destructive force.

On the other hand, if one followed the curve in the other direction, toward less taxation, there would be a point at which a drop in taxation would lead to an increase in business activity and a spurt in the economy. Lowered taxes would act as an incentive to businessmen, giving them confidence in the economy, and freeing money for investment.

[70]

Since business was up, so were profits and so was the total amount of money the government could tax, which would lead to greater sums of money flowing into the federal treasury.

According to George Gilder, who has written on the Laffer curve in *Wealth and Poverty*, the most important point about tax rates is the marginal tax rate where successively higher incomes are taxed at ever higher levels. It is the marginal tax rates, Gilder believes, "that determine the impact of a tax on motives and expectations, on ambitions and drives, on the willingness to go out and work to earn—or invest to gain—one more dollar."

If the marginal tax rates increase too rapidly; if a man believes that too much of the one more dollar he earns will go to the government, then he is unlikely to go out and earn that one more dollar. He is more likely, Gilder contends, to stay at home and enjoy the fruits of the money he has.

Thus the Laffer curve is a psychological theory as well as an economic hypothesis. It claims to have found a line at which motives and expectations can change for the better or be undermined by government intervention through taxation. The Laffer curve is also an elitist concept, for its primary emphasis is on the rich, not the middle- or low-income individual. The Laffer curve looks foremost at the wealthy because it is the wealthy who will have the capital to invest, once that capital has been freed from taxation.

In his book, *An American Renaissance* (1979), conservative congressman Jack Kemp (Republican, New York) cites an example of the destructive force of taxation. The case, which is hypothetical, involves a New York businessman who invests $1 million in a business venture. After two years of hard work, he makes a profit of $100,000. From this $100,000 profit, New York City, according to its tax laws, takes away $5,700, leaving $94,300. New York state then takes 10 percent of that, and the Internal Revenue Service takes $38,000.

The businessman now has $46,870, which he turns over to himself as a dividend. But dividends are also taxed, so

[71]

the process begins again. This time the city takes $2,015; the state, $6,728; and the IRS, $26,689—leaving the businessman with a total of $11,438, which breaks down to $5,719 a year for his effort.

With returns like this, the conservatives ask, is a businessman likely to feel encouraged to commit his capital and time? Isn't he more likely to take his million dollars and spend two years on his yacht? Or spend it on luxurious items which offer immediate enjoyment? It was with this prospect in mind that reporter Scott Burns, writing in the *Boston Herald American* on July 10, 1978, claimed "we will see more Cadillacs and Mercedes on the roads and more yachts in the water until the very day the economy falls apart."

What the high tax rates are telling Americans of all classes, the conservatives say, is not to invest in the future of America, but to find other ways of spending money. Americans now seek tax shelters to avoid paying high taxes, or invest in markets—like diamonds and gold—that offer no real increase of wealth for society.

The United States, the conservatives say, is on the negative side of the Laffer curve, far beyond the point where tax rates become self-defeating. The United States, they claim, has the most commercially destructive tax system of any capitalist country. This tax system places an enormous burden on the rich, a larger burden than the governments of Japan, West Germany, or other industrial nations place on their rich. The answer to our economic dilemma, they conclude, is obvious: a drastic cut in taxes, immediately, so that business will be stimulated and the economy will move out of its sluggishness.

To those who say that the Laffer curve is only theory, and a questionable one that may not work in practice, the Lafferites point to several cases where they believe the "Laffer effect" has worked, and worked well:

• During the 1950s the government of Taiwan undertook a series of significant tax cuts to raise the level of economic expansion. The cuts worked and led to a period of economic boom. Taiwan has continued to use tax cuts as incentives and the result has been one of the most dynamic capitalist economies on earth.

• On the advice of Arthur Laffer and Jude Wanniski, Governor Carlos Romero Barcelo of Puerto Rico cut Puerto Rico's income tax rate in 1978. He also removed two 5 percent tax surcharges. The next year, tax revenues increased by $15 million and unemployment dropped by 1.2 percent. The success of this first venture into Laffer economics led Governor Romero to further reduce taxes in 1979. In 1980 Puerto Rico enjoyed a 13.5 percent increase in revenue and an increase in employment of 100,000 people.

• In 1978 the people of California voted for Proposition 13, which offered a drastic cut in property taxes. Opponents of the tax cut predicted economic disaster, but no disaster occurred. Instead, say the conservatives, personal income in California grew at a rate 40 percent higher than elsewhere in the nation, and employment rose by 400,000. The increase in income and employment offset the loss of state income from property taxes, creating a surplus in the state treasury.

• But the example of successful Lafferite economics the Lafferites are fondest of pointing to is the Kennedy-Johnson tax cut of 1964, mentioned in chapter three. The Kennedy-Johnson bill cut the highest tax rate on investment income from 91 percent to 70 percent and offered an eventual reduction to 50 percent on the highest rate on "earned" income. Other tax rates were dropped proportionally. The result of the Kennedy-Johnson tax cut, the Lafferites note, was a major transfer of private investment from land and property into business, where investment capital could be used more creatively. The four years prior to the tax cut had seen a 27.4 percent of investment capital going to business and 38.5 percent to land and property. During the four years after the cuts, 58.6 percent of investment capital went into business and 11.2 percent into land and property. The transfer of investments, the Lafferites believe, led to an improvement of the American economy that lasted for several years.

In 1977 the Laffer curve was introduced into Congress in the form of the Tax Reduction Act of 1977, also known as the Kemp-Roth bill, because of its two sponsors, Congressman Jack Kemp and Senator William Roth. Kemp and Roth proposed to cut taxes by 30 percent over three years. Describing the bill, Representative Kemp called it "a massive behavioral modification program—an attempt to modify the behavior of the U.S. economy by altering dramatically the reward structure."

Reagan was impressed by the arguments behind the Laffer curve and by the Kemp-Roth bill and had spoken in support of both in the late 1970s. In the 1980 campaign he included a big tax cut in his economic program over the protests of some of his more traditional-minded economic advisers. But Reagan agreed with Kemp. The economy needed a significant jolt, and a large tax cut—larger than any ever undertaken before in American history—would provide that jolt.

There were also other tax measures included in the Reagan economic program in addition to the tax cut. Reagan supported a plan for accelerated depreciation of business assets and an elimination of the tax on oil "windfall" profits. He also approved the repeal of gift and estate taxes. These measures too were designed to stimulate business investment and improve the econmy.

What Is Supply-Side Economics?
Many of the conservative economists who have adopted the Laffer curve belong to what has been called the supply-side school of economics. They stress the importance of the supply side of the economy (the side which creates wealth and

production) over the demand side of the economy (the consumers and users of wealth and production).

The supply-siders believe that demand-side economics now dominates the economic thinking of the federal government and, to a large extent, private industry, to the detriment of American society. The trouble with demand-side economics, they claim, is that it is oriented toward the past. It is from past economic patterns and behavior that public demand can be studied and learned, and the future predicted. Demand-side economics assumes that what has been wanted in the past will be wanted in the future.

But this, say the supply-siders, is economic suicide. A straightjacket is placed upon economic development, forcing it into arbitrary and artificial patterns. The dynamic, ever-changing character of capitalism has been sacrificed in favor of a carefully planned and sterile system.

What happens when demand-side economics dominates the marketplace, ask the supply-siders? Diversity is lost in favor of "sure" items whose salability has been "assured." Numerous items repeat and imitate one another, giving the consumer little choice. The public learns to scoff at advertising which claims special virtues for products that it knows those products cannot have. The imaginative businessman wanting to launch a new business venture is shunned in favor of the dull studies of planners who have learned what people want from a perusal of computer printouts.

The effect of demand-side economics on government, the supply-siders say, is even more devastating than its effect on the private economy. In government, demand-side economics leads to the vast proliferation of government services which everyone seems to assume the public demands. The bureaucracy invents new demands to be fulfilled and thereby justifies its own existence and continued expansion. Politicians add to the momentum by creating new services they believe will please their constituents and assure their reelection to office.

Thus demand-side economics, according to the supply-siders, creates patterns of economic decline and stagnation. The only way to break these patterns, they argue, is to stop assuming the consumer is the central issue of economic life instead of the producers of wealth—the businessmen, capitalists, and entrepreneurs.

The supply-siders believe that supply creates demand, not the other way around. What is supplied will be consumed. To raise the level and quality of consumption one must raise the level and quality of supply. The supply-siders revive the old economic belief that supply creates demand.

Surprisingly, the supply-siders have turned to the works of John Maynard Keynes to support their theory. If rightly understood, they say, Keynes can be seen as reinforcing supply-side notions of economic behavior. Keynes, they point out, saw the individual capitalist at the center of the capitalist economy, and he regarded that capitalist's "state of confidence" as the most important source of economic development or decline.

Businessmen, Keynes recognized, "play a mixed game of skill and chance." They do not rely simply on "cold calculation" to plan future investments. Rather, they have to be confident enough in the future to be tempted to take a chance with their capital. "The *state of confidence*," he emphasized, "is a matter to which practical men always pay the closest and most anxious attention."

The supply-siders are in total agreement with Keynes on this point. The confidence of investors is central to capitalism. But where Keynes advocated enormous government expenditures to restore the confidence of businessmen and entrepreneurs during the Great Depression, the supply-siders now advocate that government play a different role. In the stagnating and declining economy of the 1970s and 1980s, the supply-siders say, the best way for government to restore entrepreneurial confidence is to cut taxes and cut back government intervention in the private sector of the economy.

George Gilder expresses the supply-side doctrine suc-
cinctly in *Wealth and Poverty*. "The only way tax policy
can reliably influence real incomes," he writes, "is by
changing the incentives of suppliers." By changing the current heavy tax burden borne by the suppliers, government
will alter their behavior. "*By altering the pattern of
rewards*," he concludes, "to favor work over leisure, investment over consumption . . . taxable over untaxable activity, government can directly and powerfully foster the
expansion of real demand and income." This, he adds, "is
the supply-side mandate."

Thus what the supply-siders want is an economy where
the businessman feels free to exercise his powers and confident enough of the rewards he will receive for his own labor
that he will work and invest. Such an economy, they warn,
does not now exist, nor will it come into existence, unless
government turns away from its efforts to plan and control,
to guide and manipulate.

The supply-side doctrine fits very closely to Reagan's
own vision of a capitalist system restored to the level of
functioning it once enjoyed. Supply-side ideas like the Laffer curve became a central part of his economic program,
and, after he became president, supply-side economists
took prominent positions in the department of the treasury,
the commerce department, and elsewhere in the government. It is now time to turn to Reagan's first months in
office and to see how he put his economic program into
practice.

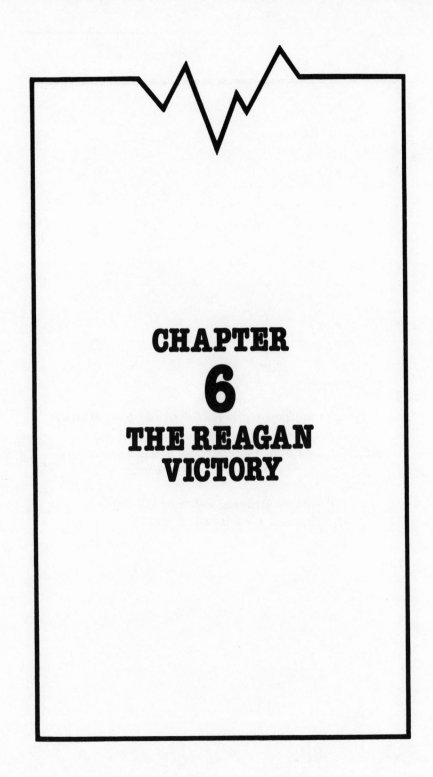

CHAPTER
6
THE REAGAN
VICTORY

We can no longer procrastinate and hope things will get better. They will not. If we do not act forcefully, and now, the economy will get worse. . . . We must alter our course.

President Reagan, February 18, 1981
in a speech to Congress.

Throughout his campaign for the presidency, Reagan promised that his economic program would be consistent and that he would pursue it in a steady and orderly fashion in order to shore up faith about the economy. "There is probably nothing," a campaign position paper said, "that undermines economic growth more than widespread uncertainty about the future actions of government. In a Reagan administration, every effort will be made to establish and begin to implement economic policy early—within the first ninety days—and then to stick to the essentials of this policy."

Reagan was as good as his word. During his first months in office, much of the program he had promised was carried out. Washington had seen nothing like it since the first dynamic one-hundred days of Roosevelt's first administration when the New Deal was begun. Now, however, a president was seeking to uproot the tradition that had begun fifty years earlier under Roosevelt and to replace it with a different philosophy of government.

The Reagan Speech

President Ronald Reagan outlined his economic plans to a joint session of Congress on February 18, 1981, less than one month after he entered office. The press quickly dubbed his program the "Reagan revolution." "The taxing power of Government," the president told Congress, "must be used to provide revenues for legitimate Government purposes. It must not be used to regulate the economy or bring about social change."

"We can no longer afford things simply because we think of them," Reagan went on. "Spending by Government must be limited to those functions which are the proper province of Government." Near the end of his speech, the president asked the members of Congress to recognize the need for a radical restructuring of the economy and to make the Reagan economic plan "our plan"—a joint endeavor by the executive and legislative branches of government.

The plan Reagan outlined to Congress had already been published in a 281-page volume entitled *America's New Beginning: A Program for Economic Recovery* and was divided into three basic components: Spending, Taxes, and Deregulation. Government spending was cut. Taxes were reduced. And deregulation was to proceed as rapidly and systematically as possible.

The Reagan cuts in government spending were impressive: $41.4 billion in the 1982 fiscal year; $123.8 billion by 1986, the last year of Reagan's present administration. For the first year, the cut of $41.4 billion broke down as follows:

- Social programs, including cuts in food stamps, medicaid, and nutrition programs . . . . $10.1 billion
- Pay and benefits, including lower pay scales for federal workers, decreased pension rates, and fewer federal employees . . . . $ 6.3 billion

[82]

- Jobs programs, such as
  EDA and CETA. . . . . $ 6.1 billion

- Subsidy cuts, including
  subsidies to the dairy
  industry, transportation,
  and the Postal Service . . . . $ 3.3 billion

- Aid to business, including
  government support for the
  synthetic fuels industry . . . . $ 3.1 billion

- Education aid, including
  student loans . . . . $ 1.6 billion

- Housing programs, including
  renter subsidies to
  low income renters . . . . $ 0.6 billion

- Foreign aid . . . . $ 0.4 billion

- Miscellaneous cuts . . . . $ 9.9 billion

The president defended his proposed cuts as equitable—
hitting everyone in America, businessman and consumer
alike, and leaving no one to carry a heavier burden. "If
misery loves company," he said the day before he delivered
his speech to Congress, "then everybody better love everybody else, because we didn't overlook anyone."

In the taxing section of his program, Reagan asked Congress to adopt the Kemp-Roth bill, instituting a 10 percent
cut in income taxes for each year over the next three years,
for a total of 30 percent. In addition, he promised to seek
more tax cuts, including a reduction of estate taxes on
farms and businesses and an end to the tax "penalty" on
working married couples. The president likewise spoke of
indexing tax rates by automatically adjusting them to offset inflation, a move that would prevent taxpayers from
moving into a higher income tax bracket when their salaries
were raised to meet inflation.

The tax program offered incentives to business.
Machinery and equipment purchased for research and

development, for instance, would get an immediate three-year tax write-off. In order to make modernization and expansion of industry easier, the Reagan tax plan allowed investments in production equipment and in other assets to generate faster tax deductions than had been possible earlier.

In the deregulation section of his program, President Reagan appointed Vice-President Bush to chair a committee that would investigate regulations that cost businesses $100 million or more to fulfill. He likewise rescinded President Carter's order of the previous year that building owners set thermostats at 65° in winter and 78° in summer. The deregulation section promised more action as the administration studied government regulations more closely.

Reagan acknowledged that his program was controversial. The members of Congress would be reluctant to make cuts in programs that might harm or anger their constituents. Other critics of his policies would call them too harsh and inhumane. But in one of the more forceful parts of his speech to Congress, the president challenged his critics:

> *Have they an alternative which offers a greater chance of balancing the budget, reducing and eliminating inflation, stimulating the creation of jobs and reducing the tax burden? And if they haven't, are they suggesting we can continue on the present course without coming to a day of reckoning?*

Even Reagan's opponents, however, seemed to admire his audacity and believed it might prove beneficial to a country that had grown too staid and cynical. Said Richard Lamm, the Democratic governor of Colorado: "We are seeing the passing of an era. The age of exuberance is over and the age of austerity is here. I endorse the goal of the compassionate shrinking of Federal government. We can spend smarter money, not bigger money."

Over at OMB

The specifics of the economic program that Reagan announced to Congress were developed at the Office of

Management and Budget (OMB), one of the executive agencies of government directly under the authority of the president. The new director of OMB, appointed by Reagan in January 1981, was David Stockman, a former two-term Republican congressman from Michigan.

Stockman seemed an ideal choice to head the important agency. Brilliant, exceedingly hard-working, and devoted to conservatism, he was only in his mid-thirties but had already made a name for himself in Republican circles. In Congress, he was known as a man who sometimes let his devotion to conservative doctrine lead him to vote against bills that might benefit his own constituents. Stockman, for instance, had been the only member of Congress from Michigan to vote against the appropriation of funds to bail out the ailing Chrysler Corporation. Chrysler provided a large number of jobs in Michigan, including Stockman's home district, but the young representative had stood by his principles and had voted to deny the corporation government funds.

Stockman had also voted against many other government programs. Now as director of OMB he would oversee cuts in many of the programs he had opposed. Stockman assumed control of OMB with the same thoroughness and ability he had displayed as a congressman. A recent convert to supply-side economics, he believed that any plan adopted by the Reagan administration should provide a jolt sufficiently strong to stimulate the economy and encourage an increase in investment.

In a memorandum written the month before he became OMB director, Stockman had outlined a course of action. "President Reagan," the memorandum said, "will inherit thoroughly disordered credit and capital markets, punishingly high interest rates and a hair-trigger market psychology poised to respond strongly to early economic policy signals in either favorable or unfavorable ways."

The responsibility of OMB would therefore be to put forth a program that "simultaneously spurs the output side of the economy and also elicits a swift downward revision of inflationary expectations in the financial markets." It was

[85]

important, Stockman believed, for the administration to act swiftly and decisively. The Reagan economic program, he contended, must be "swiftly, deftly and courageously implemented in the first six months." If the administration does not approach the implementation of its economic program in this way, Stockman warned, "Washington will quickly become engulfed in political disorder . . ."

The first item on Stockman's agenda was to develop a viable and credible budget for the president to present to the country. There were several guidelines handed down by the president that had to be followed. Reagan wanted a balanced budget by 1984, so spending cuts should be designed to meet this deadline. Similarly, Reagan had declared some parts of the budget to be "off limits" and unavailable for cuts. Defense spending, which he planned to increase significantly, was one. Another was a major part of the Social Security System.

But what did that leave that could be cut by Stockman's knife? Let us assume that the total federal budget amounts to one dollar. Out of that dollar, 48 cents goes to what are known as government "disbursements"—Social Security checks, pensions to retired government and military officers, welfare, and medical care for the aged and poor. Thirty-six cents of this 48 cents were off limits by the president's orders. That left 12 cents that *might* be cut.

Forty-eight cents of the dollar went to federal disbursements. Of the 52 remaining cents, 25 went to defense, and 10 went to pay off the interest on the national debt. Both of these expenditures were untouchable, and, it should be noted, the 25 cents for defense would soon go up, due to Reagan's defense increase. The 25 cents for defense could soon become as much as 28 or 29 cents.

That left 17 cents, 9 cents of which went to pay for the traditional operations of government—the state department, the FBI, the national parks system, and so on. The final 8 cents went to grants to state and local governments for programs as diverse as building new government buildings and aiding the handicapped. Some of this money might be cut, but how much?

[86]

Out of the one dollar, 71 cents, or perhaps as much as 75 cents if the new defense budget were taken into consideration, could not be touched. Little, if any, of the 9 cents that went to traditional operations could be cut away, so that left 16 to 20 cents that might be cut. But this 16 to 20 cents was in "politically sensitive areas"—favorite programs of powerful congressmen, programs Congress would be reluctant to cut back for other reasons, and programs in which well-organized political action groups would oppose cuts.

So the problem before Stockman was not an easy one. Moreover, he wanted the cuts to be as equitable as possible, so that one segment of society did not feel itself hurt by the cuts more than others. In developing the budget, Stockman held several meetings with the president and the various members of the cabinet, thrashing out the problems of the cuts and attempting to develop a program that was consistent, thorough, and credible.

A Change of Political Climate

First came the development of the budget, then its announcement by the president. The next step in the process was the most difficult: selling the new budget to Congress. Congress was sometimes touchy—jealous of its own power and unwilling to bow, without a fight, before the authority of the president.

Of the two houses of Congress, the Senate was the lesser problem. At the time of the Reagan landslide the previous November, the Senate had gained a majority of Republicans. Some of them might demand changes in the Reagan budget, but, in the end, party loyalty might win out over individual wishes.

The House, however, was still controlled by the Democrats. In the days after the president's speech announcing the budget, Majority Leader Tip O'Neill of Massachusetts had vowed, "We're not going to let them tear asunder programs we've built up over the years." The Congressional Black Caucus, made up of the black members of the House of Representatives, had met and issued a statement declaring its opposition to the Reagan cuts.

[87]

In March and April of 1981, however, political observers noted a change in the political climate in Washington. The president's economic program was gaining momentum, like an idea whose time has come. The Republican party, especially in the Senate, showed rare determination and unity. Senators who pursued their own interests or fought for the preservation of favorite programs were frowned upon.

In April the Senate adopted a budget proposal very similar to the one outlined by the president. Stockman, however, did not get all the cuts he had wanted. In his original budget, he had insisted upon a $752 million deduction in the funds made available to the Export-Import Bank. The Ex-Im Bank gave subsidies to major American corporations, such as Lockheed, Boeing, General Electric, Westinghouse, McDonnell Douglas, and Western Electric, so that they could compete on an even basis with Japanese and European corporations which were subsidized by their governments.

Stockman believed that the cuts in the Ex-Im Bank appropriations were needed to show the country that the Reagan administration meant to cut federal spending across the board—from government subsidies to wealthy corporations to welfare and social programs. He had kept the Ex-Im cuts in the Reagan budget in spite of opposition from some of the president's other advisers.

In the Senate, however, the large corporations mounted a lobbying campaign to restore the Stockman reductions. Lobbyists for the corporations argued that without the government subsidies the corporations could not compete successfully with foreign firms. As a result, American sales abroad would decrease, losing the companies money and placing jobs held by Americans in peril. The lobbying campaign worked. Republican senators voted to restore most of the funds Stockman had taken from the bank.

Stockman had a more difficult time with the House of Representatives than he did with the Senate. He devoted much time to appearances before House committees— whose chairmen were all Democrats who had often sponsored the programs the Reagan budget wanted to cut or eliminate—and to discussions with individual representatives, explaining what he believed to be the important features of the Reagan economic program. He did not want to lose the momentum that seemed to be pushing the Reagan economic program through Congress.

There were three groups of Democratic representatives in the House that Stockman had to deal with. First were the old-time liberals, led by Tip O'Neill, who opposed most of the cuts the Reagan administration wanted. Once the dominant force in the House, the old-time liberals were now a minority. A second group was the large number of pragmatic, moderate Democrats, open to compromise and political bargaining. While usually supportive of liberal legislation, they nevertheless recognized the popularity of the president's program. The third group was the twenty-eight conservative southern Democrats who stood closer to Reagan than they did to the liberal wing of their own party. They might in the end openly support the Republican administration's economic plans.

Representative James R. Jones was the chairman of the House Budget Committee. A moderate Democrat from Tulsa, Oklahoma, he hoped that his committee could come up with a budget that would hold the Democrats in the House together and thereby defeat the president's budget. The problem was to come up with a program of cuts acceptable to the liberals but at the same time large enough to impress the conservative Democrats. It proved to be an impossible task.

The Reagan administration concentrated on converting the southern Democrats, dubbed the "boll weevils." The boll weevils came from districts that had heavily supported Reagan in the election; they were therefore vulnerable to defeat by Republican opponents in the future. President Reagan, however, let it be known that if they supported his program, neither he nor any other Republicans would campaign against them.

Other enticements were also held out. Representative

[89]

G.V. Montgomery of Mississippi, the chairman of the House Veteran's Affairs Committee, opposed cuts that had been made in veteran's benefits. Stockman restored nearly $400 million to the budget for the staffing of veteran's hospitals, and Montgomery came over the president's side, urging other southern Democrats to do likewise.

In April President Reagan went on television to explain his economic program to the American public. He explained what he believed to be the economic crisis the country was in and stressed the importance of the quick passage of his program. The result was a large outpouring of support for the president. Members of Congress received mail from constituents supporting the Reagan program. In the end, the Reagan economic plan passed the House of Representatives with little significant modification.

The Democrats had lost; the president had won. In the "reconciliation process"—the process of arriving at a bill both the House and the Senate could agree upon—that followed, a total of more than $36 billion in cuts was approved, only $5 billion short of the cuts the president had wanted. It was an impressive victory and was due in no small measure to the work of David Stockman.

The Tax Cuts

The next major problem for the administration was the passage of its program of tax cuts. Many members of Congress, liberals and conservatives alike, questioned the wisdom of such drastic cuts in a period of inflation. They believed that the cuts would only fuel inflation and would lead to greater economic problems for the nation. Moreover, they had little faith in the promises made by supply-side economists that the tax cuts would spur the economy and would lead to greater tax revenues.

When the question of the cuts came before Congress, however, all reservations seemed to evaporate. Fears about the inflationary nature of high tax cuts were forgotten in a battle to see which party could offer the biggest cuts. The battle was spurred on by Washington's tax lobbyists who urged Democratic and Republican politicians to support cuts that favored business, banking, and other interests.

The tax bill offered by the Democrats gave businessmen the opportunity to write off investments in the first year after they were made, as well as a $7 billion tax concession for small independent oil producers. It also exempted estates under $600,000 from inheritance taxes and cut the top rates of income tax from 70 percent to 50 percent.

The administration matched the cuts made by the Democrats and then raised them. In the end, the bill adopted by Congress gave the president a 25 percent cut in income taxes over the next three years, instead of the 30 percent he had asked for. Five percent was to be cut the first year, and 10 percent for each of the two following years. The cuts for business were to be retroactive to the beginning of 1981; the cuts for individuals were to begin the last quarter of the year.

The final tax bill reduced by $750 billion the amount of revenue the federal government would take in over the next five years. It was another major victory for the administration and a victory for supply-side economics. In a short amount of time, the Reagan "revolution" had been spectacularly successful. It had begun to slow down, if not to reverse, the trend toward ever-increased government spending, a trend many believed could not be held back.

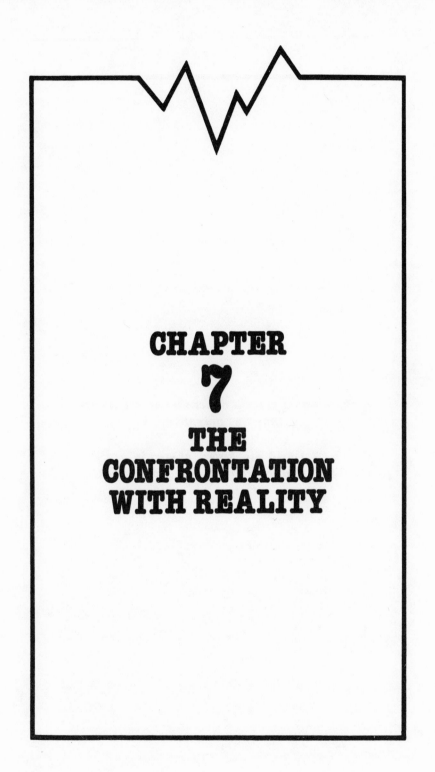

CHAPTER
7
THE
CONFRONTATION
WITH REALITY

There was a certain dimension of our theory that was unrealistic.

David Stockman, quoted in
***The Atlantic Monthly*, December, 1981.**

There was good economic news in 1981. Wall Street reacted to Reagan's election positively. The Dow Jones average went above 1,000 for the first time in four years to reach a high of 1,024 on April 27. Inflation had fallen out of the double-digit range to between 7 and 8 percent, and the administration believed it could be kept below 10 percent for the rest of the year. Economists attributed the lower inflation rates to a good wheat harvest and to a glut in the world supply of oil.

But there was also bad economic news. Over the summer, the Dow Jones average fell to 851, the lowest it had been in fifteen months, and corporate bond values reached record depths. Reacting to the news, David Jones, the chief economist for the Wall Street securities firm of Aubrey G. Lanston & Co., described the feeling on the stock market as "horrible. Prices just keep falling. It's frustration. Hopelessness."

Production likewise fell. During the first three months of 1981, U.S. production of goods and services expanded at an annual rate of 8.6 percent, but it fell rapidly in the second quarter to an annual rate of 2.4 percent. And there was little sign of improved business outlook.

The prime interest rate, which had gone down somewhat earlier in the year, rose again to 20.5 percent, causing further economic problems. Auto sales in 1981 were running 30 percent below what they had been in 1978. Home construction was expected to fall to its lowest level since 1946. By the end of September, 11,076 companies had gone bankrupt in 1981, a 42 percent rise over the same period for 1980.

One of the hardest hit major corporations was Pan American World Airways, which lost $217.6 million during the first half of 1981. But troubled too were savings and loan associations, the mainstay of home financing. Eighty five percent of the nation's savings and loan associations were losing money, and some prominent economists argued that they would need government help in order to survive.

The problem was confidence. H. James Toffey, managing director of the First Boston Corporation pointed out, "Wall Street was always scared of tax cuts without commensurate spending cuts." And Henry Kaufman of the respected Wall Street firm of Salomon Brothers publicly denounced the president's program, saying that drastic tax cuts coupled with increased defense spending was no prescription for economic improvement. Such a program, Kaufman believed, could only lead to an enormous inflation rate.

Francis Schott, chief economist for the Equitable Life Assurance Society, zeroed in on supply-side economics. "Guys like economist Art Laffer and Congressman Jack Kemp," he said, "are O.K. to have around as long as you just take note of what they say and look for the kernel of truth in it. But you don't necessarily do what they prescribe. That's just a prescription for disaster."

What Wall Street was reacting to was its fear that the Reagan economic program would result in huge deficits, in spite of the vast cuts the president had made in government spending. Wall Street computers estimated deficits ranging from $40 billion to $60 billion and more. This indicated that Reagan had not gotten federal spending under control and that still more had to be done to inspire confidence in the business community.

Balancing the Budget

At OMB, David Stockman had realized in the spring that the Reagan budget would not lead to a balanced budget. Many of the cuts the administration had succeeded in making were from a hypothetical number, where spending might go if government policies were not changed. These cuts, therefore, did not represent cuts in the "real" budget where reductions would have to be made to eliminate the "real" deficit.

As part of his original budget statement to the president, Stockman included a section he called "Chapter II." Chapter II was designed to do two things. First, it would provide increased income to the government that would offset the deficits resulting from the Reagan economic plan. Second, it would acquire additional income by eliminating tax "loopholes" enjoyed by oil interests and other corporations.

Chapter II called for an end to the oil-depletion allowance. It called for reductions in the defense budget and for a ceiling on home-mortgage deductions permitted wealthier Americans. It also called for "user fees" on yachts and other privately owned boats, and on private airplanes—another tax that would affect the rich but touch few middle-class and no poor Americans.

In addition to providing more income to cover the budget deficits, Stockman believed that Chapter II would make the Reagan economic plan more attractive to liberals and therefore would make its passage through Congress and its acceptance by the country easier. Except for the tax on yachts, however, the president did not like Chapter II and removed it from the budget program.

After failing to win approval for the inclusion of Chapter II, Stockman then had two other hopes to lessen the deficits he saw coming over the next few years. The first alternative was to convince the president that there would have to be cuts in defense. The second was that the tax cut proposed by Reagan would be cut down by Congress so that its effect on government income would not be drastic.

Stockman hoped that economic reality would force the president to realize that some sacrifice had to be made in his large defense increases if the budget were to be balanced. He proposed cuts in the range of $12 and $13 billion, only to see them whittled down by Caspar Weinberger, the secretary of defense, who urged Reagan to maintain his plans for the military. The president finally agreed to defense cuts of about $2 billion, far short of Stockman's hopes and far short of the amount needed to balance the budget.

In the last chapter, we saw the fate of Stockman's other hope to balance the budget—tax cuts. The OMB director believed that when the Reagan tax program came before Congress it would be reduced by congressmen who were concerned about the effect the cut would have on the inflation rate. The tax cut, based on the Laffer curve, was a new and untested notion and had never been tried before on the scale the president proposed. Congress, Stockman hoped, would be reluctant to allow the president to "experiment" with an economy that was already uncertain and out of sorts.

Stockman's hopes were dashed as Democrats and Republicans competed with one another to *increase* the level of the tax cut. New tax deductions were added to the program and the administration gave its approval. As a result, the government's future income was reduced, not strengthened. The problem of balancing the budget seemed more elusive than ever.

Confrontation with Congress
But where were the needed budget cuts going to come from? Stockman now turned to Social Security, medical benefits, and other similar social programs. The cuts would have to come from these programs, but where? President Reagan had promised the country that his spending cuts would never destroy what he called a "safety net" for the

truly needy, and further reductions in social benefits might be regarded by the public as an attempt to go back on that promise.

Moreover, any new cuts in those programs would be *in addition* to the cuts which had already been proposed to Congress and which Congress approved after long discussion in April and May. Stockman had been careful to point out when he submitted the first budget to Congress that there were certain programs that were slated for future reductions in addition to the reductions in the original budget. Nevertheless, he knew that Congress would be unhappy if the administration came forward demanding additional cuts in programs that the senators and representatives believed they had already settled.

Stockman's fears proved true. In May, not long after it had achieved its first victory in Congress and saw the passage of the spending cuts, the Reagan administration proposed new changes in the Social Security Act. Among the changes the administration wanted were a major reduction in benefits granted those who retired early at sixty-two and a three-month deferral of the cost-of-living adjustment for all Social Security recipients, which meant that over the next three months Social Security checks would not rise to meet inflation.

The proposals caused alarm and a widespread reaction. Groups representing elderly Americans protested that the plans were unfair. Social Security beneficiaries sent a deluge of letters to their congressional representatives denouncing the changes. Early retirement at sixty-two was popular; more than 64 percent of Americans eligible for early retirement in the 1970s took advantage of that privilege.

The Senate, hoping to alleviate the fears of the elderly, voted 96 to 0 to reject the administration's proposals. The message was clear: the Social Security program could not be tampered with. The Reagan economic program would have to look elsewhere for further spending cuts. It was the first confrontation between the president and Congress, but there would be more.

[99]

By fall of 1981 estimates of the budget deficit had grown considerably. Some projections spoke in terms of a deficit of $60 or $80 billion for fiscal 1982. New OMB figures foresaw deficits of more than $100 billion in 1982 and of more than $150 billion in 1984. The estimates contributed to further uncertainty on Wall Street and in the economy.

On September 24 President Reagan announced a program of additional spending cuts and tax measures his administration planned to take. He wanted a 12 percent across-the-board cut in federal programs except for defense. The 12 percent would affect programs already cut by the spring budget, as well as programs previously untouched. The president also announced a number of "revenue enhancers" (small tax increases) that would add $3 billion to the treasury in fiscal 1982 and would help offset the projected deficits.

Congress balked at the new requests. Many Republicans felt betrayed by the administration and particularly by Stockman. They thought the "battle of the budget" had been fought and won, and they did not want to fight the battle all over again. Conservative Republican Trent Lott, a senator from Mississippi, believed that Congress was bound to honor the commitments it had already made and not launch off into a new spree of spending cuts.

Liberal Republicans in the Senate, known as "gypsy moths," announced that they would resist the new 12 percent across-the-board cuts unless defense spending received the same scrutiny as the other programs. Liberal and moderate Democrats in the House joined in denouncing the new cuts, and even the position of the conservative southern Democrats, the boll weevils, was in question. Clearly, the Reagan economic program had lost its momentum.

On October 1, President Reagan warned that he would veto any legislation from Congress that might "bust the budget" he planned for the country. One week later, he announced that he would use his presidential authority to "defer" monies already appropriated by Congress for expenditure at a later date. The president had drawn the line. If Congress refused to submit to his new requests, he would use his power to keep federal spending down.

If the president vetoed legislation passed by Congress, it would be returned to Congress for further consideration until a bill was produced that was acceptable to Reagan. A presidential veto could be overturned if two-thirds of Congress voted to overturn it, but it was unlikely that Reagan's opponents could muster that many votes.

The threat of deferral of funds particularly angered many members of Congress. Deferral is a legal procedure in which a president announces to Congress the specific spending programs he plans to withhold and why. A majority of either house can then vote to override the deferral and if the deferral is rejected, the president must then spend the funds.

The problem was that deferral can be a lengthy process, and the president threatened to defer funds in at least *eight hundred* programs, bogging the business of the House down in the process of deferral. House Speaker Tip O'Neill charged that the deferral announcement amounted to a "deliberate act . . . to break commitments" the administration had already made. Other liberal representatives said that Reagan was repeating mistakes made ten years earlier by President Nixon when Nixon attempted to "impound" funds that had been appropriated by Congress and to prevent their expenditure. The impoundment of funds was an excessive use of presidential authority then, they claimed, just as Reagan's threat of deferral was now.

In the midst of the struggle between Congress and the president in the fall of 1981 came two presidential announcements that revealed setbacks in the Reagan economic program. First, Reagan admitted that it would be impossible for his administration to balance the federal budget by 1984. Then, a few days later, he acknowledged that the economy had entered a recession.

Both admissions must have been difficult for an administration that had thus far proved so dynamic and forceful. In his debate the year before with Independent party candidate John Anderson, Reagan had said, "I believe the budget can be balanced by 1982 or 1983." And as late as May 1981, he had reiterated his faith in supply-side economics and its ability to stimulate the economy and increase tax revenues. "As revenues continue to rise while we keep the brakes on federal spending," Reagan said, "we can certainly balance the budget; in fact, we expect a small surplus in 1984." Now those hopes had to be abandoned.

The acknowledgment of the recession was more serious. Reagan at first thought the recession would be slight, but soon had to reassess this opinion. Two weeks after his acknowledgment, figures released by the government showed that the recession would be deeper than he had predicted. The nation's output would fall by an annual rate of 3 to 5 percent over the next few months, the rate of real economic growth would decrease, and unemployment would rise.

In January Reagan had predicted real economic growth, adjusted for inflation, would be 4.2 percent from 1981 to 1982. In July this prediction had been scaled down to 3.4 percent. Now Reagan said it would be 1 percent. In July the president's economic forecasters had said unemployment would fall from 7.7 percent in 1981 to 7.0 percent in 1982. Now they believed it would be much higher in early 1982, perhaps more than 8 percent.

On November 6, at a Republican fund-raising dinner in New York City, the president stated his firm belief in his economic program. The administration, he said, was not going "to push the panic button" because of the bad economic news. His economic program, he declared, would stay on course and not be altered. It was still a very new program, which had not had time to be proven right or wrong. "If you listen closely," he said, "you can hear the spank and then the cry" of its birth.

Five days later, on November 11, the president once again defended his program. "This government," he said, "must stiffen its spine and not throw in the towel on our fight to get federal spending under control." Reagan, however, did make one concession to Congress. The cuts he had wanted in programs that make direct payments to individuals—welfare and social programs—would be postponed until January. But he once again asked Congress to approve a 12 percent cut in other programs.

The confrontation between Congress and the president continued into the late fall of 1981. Several deadlines were passed before Congress finally agreed upon a program that was acceptable to President Reagan. The cuts the president received were far short of the ones he wanted, assuring a large budget deficit in fiscal 1982.

The prospects for the Reagan economic program in 1982 are not good, because 1982 is an election year, when one-third of the Senate and all the members of the House of Representatives will stand for election. None of them are likely to support legislation which might prove unpopular. Congress in 1982 is likely to prove more cautious and recalcitrant than it was in the last months of 1981.

The Stockman Confession

While the battle between Congress and the president was raging, an article entitled "The Education of David Stockman" appeared in the December 1981 issue of *The Atlantic Monthly*.* Written by *Washington Post* reporter William Greider, the article caused an immediate sensation throughout the country. Greider had met with Stockman on several occasions throughout 1981 over breakfast at Washington's Hays-Adams Hotel. Candidly and honestly, Stockman had spoken of his problems at OMB and the ordeal of putting the Reagan economic program through Congress.

Stockman told Greider that he had known as early as January 1981 that the president's economic plan was in trouble. The proposed budget cuts were not sufficient to balance the budget, given the president's planned increase in defense spending and the tax cuts. When he first fed the figures through the OMB computers, he said, the deficits

---

*The December issue went to subscribers in early November and appeared on newsstands in the middle of the month. It therefore appeared precisely at the right time to add to Reagan's difficulties with Congress.

revealed were enormous. But he had then changed the computers to return a more optimistic report and had brought the deficit down.

Moreover, Stockman went on, the president's policymakers had known the plan was inadequate and would not achieve its predicted effects, but had still conveyed feelings of confidence to the public. The problem, he believed, was that the administration had had to work too quickly to meet deadlines. It had wanted to gain political momentum and to be on top of things in order to accomplish its goals quickly and powerfully.

The budget, Stockman confessed, "was put together so fast that it probably should have been put together differently." He went on:

The reason we did it wrong—not wrong, but less than optimum—was that we said, Hey, we have to get a program out fast. And when you decide to put a program of this breadth and depth out fast, you can only do so much. We were working in a twenty- or twenty-five-day time frame, and we didn't think it all the way through. We didn't add up all the numbers. We didn't make all the thorough, comprehensive calculations about where we really needed to come out and how much to put on the plate the first time, and so forth.

The budget finally produced by OMB, Stockman said, was derived from a list of things he had "always been carrying of things to be done, rather than starting the other way and asking, What is the overall fiscal policy required to reach the target?"

OMB operated at a frenetic pace, Stockman admitted, "juggling details, pushing people, and going from one session to another, trying to cut housing programs here and rural electrification there, and we were doing it so fast, we didn't know where we were ending up for sure." The budget-makers, he concluded, "should have designed those pieces to be more compatible."

*But the pieces were moving on independent tracks—
the tax program, where we were going on spending,
and the defense program, which was just a bunch of
numbers written on a piece of paper. And it didn't
quite mesh.*

How did OMB and the administration get by with the
appearance of being on top of things? Because, Stockman
claimed, "the novelty of all these budget reductions" had
everyone fooled for a while.

In the play of power politics in Washington, Stockman
said, it was the "weak clients" who lost out in the budget-
cutting process. The weak clients had no one to represent
their interests, while the wealthy corporations and well-
heeled groups had more than enough clout to protect their
interests from the cuts. "Unorganized groups," Stockman
pointed out, "can't play this game." Only the groups who
"know how to make themselves heard" can win.

Stockman, once a supply-sider, now had his doubts.
"Laffer," he said, "sold us a bill of goods . . . Laffer
wasn't wrong—he didn't go far enough." The supply-siders, Stockman explained, were "naive" and missed a
"whole dimension" of budget planning. "You don't stop
inflation without some kind of dislocation." Yet the supply-
side economists have "created this nonpolitical view of the
economy, where you are going to have big changes and
abrupt turns," a "happy vision of this world of growth and
no inflation with no pain."

The world simply doesn't work that way, Stockman
implied. Supply-side economics offered the wrong "atmo-
spherics" for the Reagan economic plan. It did not show the
economic difficulties that would follow a major change in
the government's role in economic life, but offered an
unreal promise of economic boom and prosperity.

The Kemp-Roth bill, Stockman continued, was "always
a Trojan horse to bring down the top rate" of taxation. The
bill proposed to bring down all tax rates, but its real purpose, Stockman claimed, was to help the rich. Other tax

brackets were brought down merely to make the bill "palatable as a political matter." Supply-side economics, he concluded, is really "trickle-down theory" in a new guise.

After Stockman's confession had caused a nationwide sensation, the young director of OMB submitted his resignation to President Reagan and went on television to explain the article. Stockman reiterated his faith in the Reagan economic program and urged its adoption by Congress. He likewise stated his belief that it was the only program that offered hope for economic improvement and genuine change.

But the damage had been done and Stockman's future at OMB was uncertain. President Reagan rejected Stockman's resignation, but powerful political figures in the Republican party wondered aloud about the ability of a man who had so candidly revealed his doubts about the program to carry it to Congress and convince Congress of its effectiveness.

What Stockman's doubts revealed was that there were two different—and perhaps irreconcilable—economic theories at work in the Reagan program. One was a traditional conservative policy of economic recovery advocating a balanced budget, achieved through spending cuts without a drop in taxation. The other was supply-side economics with its promise of recovery through huge cuts in taxation.

Stockman, a convert to supply-side economics, had tried to balance the two approaches during his early days at OMB. He found it an impossible task, and slowly lost his faith in the "magic" of supply-side economics, coming to rely instead on the approach offered by traditional conservatives. Economic recovery, he now believed, would have to come from "fiscal integrity" and a balanced budget, not from the promises of the supply-siders.

The future of the Reagan economic program will depend on the success of the supply-side theory. If the tax cuts do generate an economic boom, then the supply-side part of the Reagan program will be kept. If there is no boom, then supply-side economics and the huge tax cut will be dropped in favor of the traditional conservatives' approach.

CHAPTER
8
CRITICS RIGHT
AND LEFT

I believe we can embark on a new age of reform in this country and an era of national renewal, an era that will reorder the relationship between citizen and government, that will make government again responsive to people, that will revitalize the values of family, work, and neighborhood and that will restore our private and independent social institutions. These institutions always have served as both buffer and bridge between the individual and the state—and these institutions, not government, are the real sources of our economic and social progress of our people.

Ronald Reagan in 1980.

The creation of the society described above is the real force behind the Reagan economic plan. Such a society once existed, he claims, but is in a state of deterioration, and only the proper cures—hard work, free enterprise, and individual initiative—can restore it. A properly revitalized America, Reagan tells us, will once again be powerful enough to assume its traditional place in the economic and social affairs of the world.

But will the Reagan economic plan work? Numerous critics believe that it won't. Presented here are the views of two—one on the right, one on the left—who find the Reagan plan inadequate and incapable of achieving what it hopes to achieve.

On the Right

Peter G. Peterson is the chairman of the board of Lehman Brothers Kuhn Loeb and widely regarded as one of the two or three most articulate economic analysts in the United States. A former secretary of commerce in the Nixon administration in 1972, he believes that the Reagan economic plan starts in the right direction, but does not go nearly far enough.

Peterson congratulates Reagan on offering the country a new look at economics. The old economic patterns, he agrees, had become shopworn and had long proved detrimental to economic health and growth. But the Reagan plan, he fears, as fresh and new as it is, does not analyze the problem of American economic sluggishness successfully, nor does it offer a solution that is likely to increase productivity.

First, Peterson turns to the economic success of Japan and West Germany. Between 1970 and 1979, he points out, Japan and West Germany did far better than the United States economically even though both countries have far more severe problems of energy and natural resources than the United States does.

By 1980 Japan, with an economy half the size of America's, was spending more in absolute terms on plant improvement and equipment than the United States. During the 1970s Japan and West Germany doubled their output of scientists and engineers, while the American output *declined*. In the same period, the number of patents for new inventions issued to U.S. companies declined by 10 percent, while those issued to Japanese companies increased by 372 percent.

Clearly, Peterson concludes, the United States can no longer compete creatively and productively with these two economies. What does he believe can be done about the American economy? He believes we need to sink between 3 and 5 percent of the GNP into "productivity-enhancing investments"—that is, into plants and equipment and research and development.

The Reagan tax cuts, he argues, do not do this because they are insufficient and because they are not directed against the proper economic targets. Of the tax cuts Reagan has made, Peterson maintains, only 22 percent are designed to spur investment and this is far from enough to allow America to compete with the far more dynamic economies of the other industrialized, capitalist nations.

The United States, Peterson claims, takes a greater share of its revenues from taxes that hurt business than do the governments of Japan, West Germany, France, or the United Kingdom. Indeed, he goes on, those nations have tax programs that are specifically designed to relieve business and provide proper stimuli for expansion and improvement. Yet the Reagan economic program has not followed their example and provided similar incentives. Its plans are still too disorganized, too misdirected, and too cautious.

Peterson also criticizes the Reagan spending cuts. Our major government programs, he believes, must grow at a rate "significantly less than the growth of the GNP"—and this means government programs such as Social Security, medicare, and medicaid. Such programs occupy ever-increasingly large segments of the GNP because they are indexed to rise with inflation. President Reagan was wrong, Peterson argues, to exempt the major portions of these programs from budget cuts.

Thus Peterson's vision of an adequate economic program is one far more carefully planned and controlled than the Reagan economic program. It is also far more austere in its attitude toward spending cuts. Peterson believes that half-measures won't work because they won't root out the problem of a government that spends too much and taxes its business and industry at an unreasonable rate.

On the Left

MIT professor Emma Rothschild writes on economics for *The New York Review of Books*. In an article entitled "Reagan and the Real America," which appeared in the February 5, 1981 issue of that journal, she concluded that the Reagan economic program was not only wrongheaded, it was also potentially dangerous for the United States.

Rothschild rejects Reagan's vision of an American "spirit" which is "still there, ready to blaze into life" given the proper stimulation as pure rhetoric. The Reagan plan, she

[111]

notes, depends "on the assumption of rapid economic growth." For "only then would tax revenues be equal to Mr. Reagan's extravagant claims," only then would the president be able to pay for his defense budget and make up the losses in revenue due to the tax cuts.

"But such accelerated growth seems unlikely," Rothschild claims. The world economic outlook is uncertain and economic signs point toward a recession in 1981–1982. A recession, she adds, that has been heralded by the rapid increase of the number of people looking for jobs in the European Community and by a downturn in industrial production in the five major capitalist economies in 1980.

Since the oncoming recession makes it unlikely that Reagan will be able to pay for his economic program, it is likely, Rothschild goes on, to be "wildly inflationary." But it is likely to be wildly inflationary for other reasons too. The Reagan economic program, she believes, is intimately tied to Reagan's increase in defense spending, and vast increases in defense spending have always proved inflationary. Both the Korean War and the Vietnam War military buildups began in periods of low inflation and ended in periods of high inflation, she points out.

Rothschild also argues that the Reagan economic program will put people out of work. The enormous budget cuts, she says, will end jobs in service-related industries like nursing homes and are likely to affect numerous other industries as well. Increased defense spending in the 1980s, she maintains, will not create more jobs, because Reagan's military budget is directed toward weapons like nuclear missile systems, submarines, and planes—programs which require scientists and engineers, but relatively few manufacturing workers.

With the prospect of rampant inflation all but inevitable and unemployment on the rise, what solution is the Reagan administration likely to turn to? Rothschild believes that it will fall back on what she calls "the conventional conservative remedy of recession"—"control the money supply, increase taxes (or limit tax cuts), hack with ever greater frenzy at nonmilitary government spending."

"Such conservative orthodoxy," Rothschild concludes, "could bring about the second great danger of the Reagan economic policy, namely a collapse of employment throughout the economy." How can the United States avoid this catastrophe? By careful economic planning based on the realities of American society as it exists today. The Reagan economic policy, Rothschild implies, should be based less on a conservative vision of how America should work, and more on the way it does work.

Will "Reaganomics" work? That is the question conservative Peterson and liberal Rothschild ask of Reagan's economic plan, and both conclude that it won't. Their views, however, are economic predictions and economic predictions are notoriously fallible and subject to change and reappraisal. Other economists, more tolerant of experimentation, might agree with Giorgio La Malfa, Italy's budget minister, who said: "Supply-side theory is an important new departure, which deserves to be fully tried."

Like the New Deal, Reagan's economic program is a new departure for America and like the New Deal it shows America's amazing ability for change and innovation. It will not be the final answer, but it is an answer. "Some people are frustrated because we don't see instant recovery," President Reagan commented in October 1981. "We can't be stampeded now by frustration or fear. We have to stay on a steady long-term course."

SUGGESTED FURTHER READING

On Ronald Reagan see Bill Boyarsky, *Ronald Reagan, His Life & Rise to the Presidency** (New York: Random House, 1981); and *Reagan, the Man, the President** (New York: Macmillan, 1980), by a team of five *New York Times* correspondents.

Milton Friedman's *Capitalism and Freedom* (Chicago: University of Chicago Press, 1962) is an articulate defense of conservative economics. More on the popular level is Milton and Rose Friedman's *Free to Choose, A Personal Statement** (New York: Harcourt Brace Jovanovich, 1980).

Supply-side economics is defended in George Gilder's *Wealth and Poverty* (New York: Basic Books, 1981); Jude Wanniski's *The Way the World Works* (New York: Basic Books, 1978); and Arther Laffer and Jan Seymour's *The Economics of the Tax Revolt* (New York: Harcourt Brace Jovanovich, 1979).

*An asterisk (*) denotes a book of interest to the younger reader.

On the liberal side is Robert Lekachman's excellent guide to the thought of Keynes, *The Age of Keynes* (New York: Random House, 1966); Robert Heilbroner's *Beyond Boom and Crash* (New York: W.W. Norton & Company, 1978); and *The Galbraith Reader* (Ipswich, Mass.: Gambit, 1977), a collection of Galbraith's writings.

*Time** magazine carries well-informed economic commentary, as do *Newsweek** and *U.S. News and World Report.**

INDEX

Affluent Society, The, 40
Agricultural Adjustment Act, 22
American Dream, the, 18, 38
American Renaissance, An, 71
Americans for Democratic Action (ADA), 9
America's New Beginning: A Program for Economic Recovery, 82
Anderson, John, 13–14, 16, 101
Atlantic Monthly, The, 94, 103

Barcelo, Carlos Romero, 73
Beyond Boom and Crash, 6–7
Boston Herald American, 72
Bureau of the Budget, 35
Burns, Scott, 72
Bush, George, (Vice President), 84

Capitalism, 6–8, 23, 30, 32, 44, 52–53, 112

Carter, Jimmy, (President), 8–11, 13–14, 49, 84
Catells, Manuel, 6
Cheney, Richard, 70
Chrysler Corporation, 5, 85
Civil Works Administration (CWA), 22
Civilian Conservation Corps (CCC), 21
Cold War, the, 26
Communism, 6, 23, 32
Congress, U.S., 8–9, 13, 34–35, 74, 82–85, 87–90, 97–103, 106
Congressional Black Caucus, 87
Conscience of a Conservative, The, 38
Conservatism, 10–11, 13, 19, 22–23, 31, 36, 40, 42, 45–51, 53, 69, 72, 85, 89–90, 100, 106, 112–113

Council of Economic Advisers, 35

Crash of '79, The, 6

de Combret, Francois, 7
Defense spending, 12, 14, 68–69, 86–87, 97–98, 100, 103, 105, 112
Deferral of funds, 100–101
Democratic Party, 10, 20, 34, 38, 88–91, 98
Depression, Great, 17–20, 24–25, 30–31, 33, 36, 76
Depressions, 18, 31
d'Estaing, Giscard, (President of France), 7
"Double-digit inflation," 4
Dow Jones Industrial Average, 95

Economic boom of the 1960s, 45
Economic Crisis and American Society, The, 6
Economic crisis of the 1970s, 3–8, 45–46
Economics and the Public Purpose, 40
"Education of David Stockman, The?" 103
Education, Department of, 12
Eisenhower, Dwight, (President), 35–37, 45, 68
Elementary and Secondary Education Act, 39
Emergency Banking Act, 21
Emergency Farm Mortgage Act, 22
Energy, Department of, 12
Erdman, Paul, 6
Export-Import Bank, 88

Fair Deal, 36
Federal Emergency Relief Act, 22
Federal Reserve Board, 69

Federal Trade Commission, 48
Feldstein, Martin, 49
Fiscal year, 9
Ford, Gerald, (President), 42, 70
France, 5, 7
Free to Choose, 51
Friedman, Milton and Rose, 51
Future While It Happened, The, 35

Galbraith, John Kenneth, 40–41, 68
General Accounting Office (GAO), 12
General Agreement on Tariffs and Trade (GATT), 7
General Motors Company, 4
General Theory of Employment, Interest and Money, The, 29, 66
Gilder, George, 6–7, 44, 51–53, 71, 77
Glass-Steagall Banking Act, 22
Gold standard, 22, 32
Goldwater, Barry, 38, 45, 68
Great Society, the, 37, 39, 41–42, 48
Greenspan, Alan, 67
Greider, William, 103
Gross National Product (GNP), 18, 110–111

Head Start, 39
Health, Education and Welfare, Department of (HEW), 12, 37, 42
Heilbroner, Robert, 6–8
Hobbs, Charles, 47
Hoover, Herbert, (President), 17–21, 25
House of Representatives, 87–90, 100. *See also* Congress
Housing and Urban Development, Department of (HUD), 48

Inflation, 3–5, 8–9, 11, 17, 46, 83–84, 90, 95, 98–99, 105, 111–112
Interest rates, 5, 8, 85, 96

Japan, 5, 72, 110–111
Job Corps, 39
Johnson, Lyndon, (President), 9, 38–40, 42, 45, 48
Jones, David, 95
Jones, James R., 89

Kaufman, Henry, 96
Kemp, Jack, 71, 74, 96
Kemp-Roth bill, 13, 74, 83, 105
Kennedy, John, (President), 38
Kennedy-Johnson tax cut of 1964, 73
Keynes, John Maynard, 29, 32, 66, 76
    economic theories of, 30–35, 37–38, 42, 45, 68
Korean War, 112

Laffer, Arthur, 70, 73, 96, 105
Laffer Curve, 69–74, 77, 98
La Malfa, Giorgio, 113
Lamm, Richard, 84
Liberalism, 9, 14, 26, 38, 50–51, 89–90, 97, 100–101
Lott, Trent, 100
Lubell, Samuel, 35

Mandate for Change, 36
Marxism, 7–8, 32
Maximum Security Act, 34–35
Mellon, Andrew, 19
Montgomery, G.V., 89–90
Murphy, Thomas A., 4

National Resources Planning Board (NRPB), 33–34
New Bill of Rights, 34

New Deal, the, 17, 20–26, 29, 33–34, 36–38, 41, 45, 48–49, 81, 113
New Industrial State, The, 40
New York City, 5
Nixon, Richard, (President), 9, 42, 101, 109–110

Office of Economic Opportunity (OEO), 38–39
Office of Management and Budget (OMB), 33, 84–85, 97–98, 100, 103–106
Office of Price Administration (OPA), 33
O'Neill, Tip, (House Speaker), 87, 89, 101

Pan American World Airways, 96
Peterson, Peter G., 109–111, 113
Presidential campaign of 1980, 8, 10–14, 67, 81
Prime interest rate, 96
Prime lending rate, 5
Public Interest, The, 49
Puerto Rico, 73

"Reagan and the Real America," 111
"Reagan revolution, the," 82, 91
Recession, 101–102, 112
Republican Party, 10, 19, 36, 38, 67, 85, 87–89, 91, 98, 100, 102, 106
Revenue Act of 1935, 23
Road to Serfdom, 51
Rogers, Will, 20
Roosevelt, Franklin, (President), 17, 20–21, 24–26, 29, 32, 35–36, 38, 42, 49, 81
Roth, William, 74
Rothschild, Emma, 111–113

"Safety net," 98–99
Samuelson, Paul, 33
Schott, Francis, 96
Schultz, George, 67
Senate, 87–88, 99–100
  See also Congress
Smith, Alfred, 20–21
Social Security, 23, 34, 36–37,
  39, 68, 86, 98–99, 111
Socialism, 32, 51–52
Soviet Union, 12, 32
"Stagflation," 4
Stock Market crash of 1929, 18
Stockman, David, (Budget Di-
  rector), 85–90, 94, 97–100,
  103–106
Supply-side economics, 11, 14,
  68, 74–77, 85, 91, 96, 102,
  105–106, 113

Taxes, 10–11, 13, 23, 31, 35, 69,
  71–73, 76, 82
  cuts in, 13–14, 38, 70, 90–91,
    98, 103, 105–106, 110, 112
Tax Reduction Act of 1977.
  See Kemp-Roth bill
"Tight-money" policy, 5
Toffey, H. James, 96
"Trickle-down" theory, 20, 40,
  106
Truman, Harry, (President), 35–
  37

Tumler, Jan, 7–8

Unemployment, 3, 5–6, 13, 17–
  19, 25–26, 49, 102, 112
Upward Bound, 39

Vietnam War, 39, 112
Volunteers in Service to America (VISTA), 39
von Hayek, Friedrich, 51

Wall Street, 95–96, 100
Wall Street Journal, 48, 68,
  70
Wanniski, Jude, 50, 70, 73
War Production Board, 33
Washington Post, 103
Way the World Works, The,
  50
Wealth and Poverty, 6, 44, 51,
  53, 71
Weinberger, Caspar, (Defense
  Secretary), 98
Welfare, 12, 47–48
Welfare Industry, The, 47
"Welfare state," 17, 50, 52
West Germany, 5, 72, 110–111
Work Projects Administration
  (WPA), 22
World War I, 19
Word War II, 3, 25–26, 29, 33–
  34

DATE DUE			
MAR 11 86			
MAY 27 86			